Michael Brady

# NORDIC TOURING AND
# CROSS COUNTRY SKIING

FIFTH REVISED EDITION

DREYER

Oslo

Nordic Touring and Cross Country Skiing
First edition 1966; second printing 1968; third printing 1969.
Second edition 1970; second printing 1971.
Third revised edition 1971; second printing 1972; third printing 1974.
Fourth revised edition 1977; second printing 1978.
Fifth revised edition 1979
Library of Congress Catalog Card No. 77-77159
ISBN 82-09-01781-0

Published by Dreyers Forlag, Arbiens gate 7,
Oslo 2, Norway

Printed in the United States of America 1979 by

Port City Press, Inc., New York, Philadelphia and Baltimore
Typesetting by Combine Graphics Corp., New York

# CONTENTS

# PREFACE

This book is devoted to the essentials of cross country skiing, the winter sport that offers something for everyone.

For novices, cross country skiing is ideal because it is less expensive, safer and easier than Alpine skiing to learn to the point where it can be enjoyed. There is no "right" age for enjoying cross country. Anyone who walks or hikes can learn its basic walk-like movements.

For outdoorsmen and backpackers, cross country skiing is the key to year-round activity. With good touring equipment and technique, one can travel much faster than on snowshoes. For Alpine skiers, cross country adds a new dimension to the sport. The terrain the non-touring skier misses can never be equaled, no matter how many downhill runs are made. For athletes, cross country ski racing is the most comprehensive of all international skiing events. More Winter Olympic medals are awarded for cross country racing than for any other winter sport. For instructors, cross country lends itself superbly to teaching because it builds on what pupils can do: walk. For the handicapped, cross country skiing is one of the more readily enjoyable and easily learned of winter sports.

The first edition of this book appeared in January 1966, a time when cross country skiing was little known as a winter recreation outside of the Nordic countries. This fifth edition reflects not only the extensive changes in cross country in the last decade, but also the sport's worldwide coming of age.

To John Fry, editorial director of SKI Magazine, goes the credit for encouraging and originally publishing much of the first edition's material as a series of articles in SKI.

Many of the changes in the fourth and fifth editions arose out of discussions with Ned Gillette. Marianne Hadler thoroughly reviewed the text and contributed to this edition's content in addition to supplying the skills shown in many of the illustrations. Photographer Frits Solvang is again responsible for most of the photographs. Artist Odd Pettersen produced the drawings. And to the many others unnamed here—coaches and pupils, readers and critics—sincere thanks.

M. Michael Brady
Oslo, June 1979

6

# FREE CATALOG

Fill out and mail this card to receive a
free catalog of all Wilderness Press publications.

Our catalog includes:

- books for hikers, backpackers, climbers, skiers, bicyclists and other outdoor enthusiasts

- a wide selection of hiking guides to the Western states and the Hawaiian Islands

- maps of popular hiking areas in California

- beautiful hardback editions for gifts and personal collections

name _____

address _____

city_____

state/zip_____

# WHAT IT IS

The grace and speed of the cross country racer, the distance-covering, steady stride of polar explorers, and the easy pace of weekend touring groups all share a common skiing technique now known as cross country, the most ancient, most recently re-discovered winter sport.

Four-thousand-year-old wall carvings in arctic Norway attest to the age of skiing, which began in and spread out from the Nordic countries. In the latter half of the 19th Century, "Snowshoe Thompson," from Norway's Telemark region, brought skis to California when his countrymen were introducing skiing in central Europe. While skiing retained its original character in the Nordic countries, the central Europeans developed their own form for pleasure skiing, suited to their steep Alpine slopes. This trend was furthered by the development of lifts to serve Alpine ski hills. Now there are two forms of skiing, Nordic and Alpine. They differ in purpose, technique, and equipment. Nordic skiing comprises recreational and competitive cross country skiing, and ski jumping. Alpine skiing comprises recreational and competitive downhill skiing.

Until recently, most Americans, Canadians, Englishmen, Australians and Central Europeans were familiar only with Alpine skiing. The situation is now different. Sparked by a renaissance in the early 1970's, cross country skiing is now as much a part of winter as is snow itself. One of the reasons is perhaps the joy of cross country: it can be done anywhere there is snow.

Cross country can also be enjoyed in many ways. Most skiers prefer cross country ski areas, of which there are now more than 500 in the USA and Canada, and literally thousands in Europe and Scandinavia, most with marked trails and prepared tracks. Some skiers elect solitude, preferring to make cross country an adventure in untracked snow. Still others compete. Cross country racing, known as "Langlauf" in German and "langrenn" in Norwegian, is a ski race similar to distance running, the standard distances being from five kilometers (three miles) to 50 kilometers (31 miles). The pace is fast, with usual times over five kilometer courses being about 16 minutes, and about two hours and 40 minutes over 50 km courses. At the international level, cross country racing is king. Even the prestigious Winter Olympics has more cross country events than any other sport: there are four men's and four women's cross country events plus two in biathlon (cross country racing and shooting) and the Nordic combined (cross country racing and ski jumping).

But cross country racing isn't just for top athletes. Each winter, citizens' races, low-key competitions divided into classes for racers and recreational skiers, are run in all skiing countries. Sweden's Vasaloppet, started in 1922, can well claim to be not only the oldest citizens' ski race but also the world's largest race of any kind: each year 10,000 or more skiers enter the 85.5 km (53 mile) event. From the Paddy Pallin Classic in Australia, to Germany's many Volkslanglauf, to the Canadian Ski Marathon and US events such as Wisconsin's American Birkebeiner, citizens' racing is now one of the most popular forms of competition for recreational skiers.

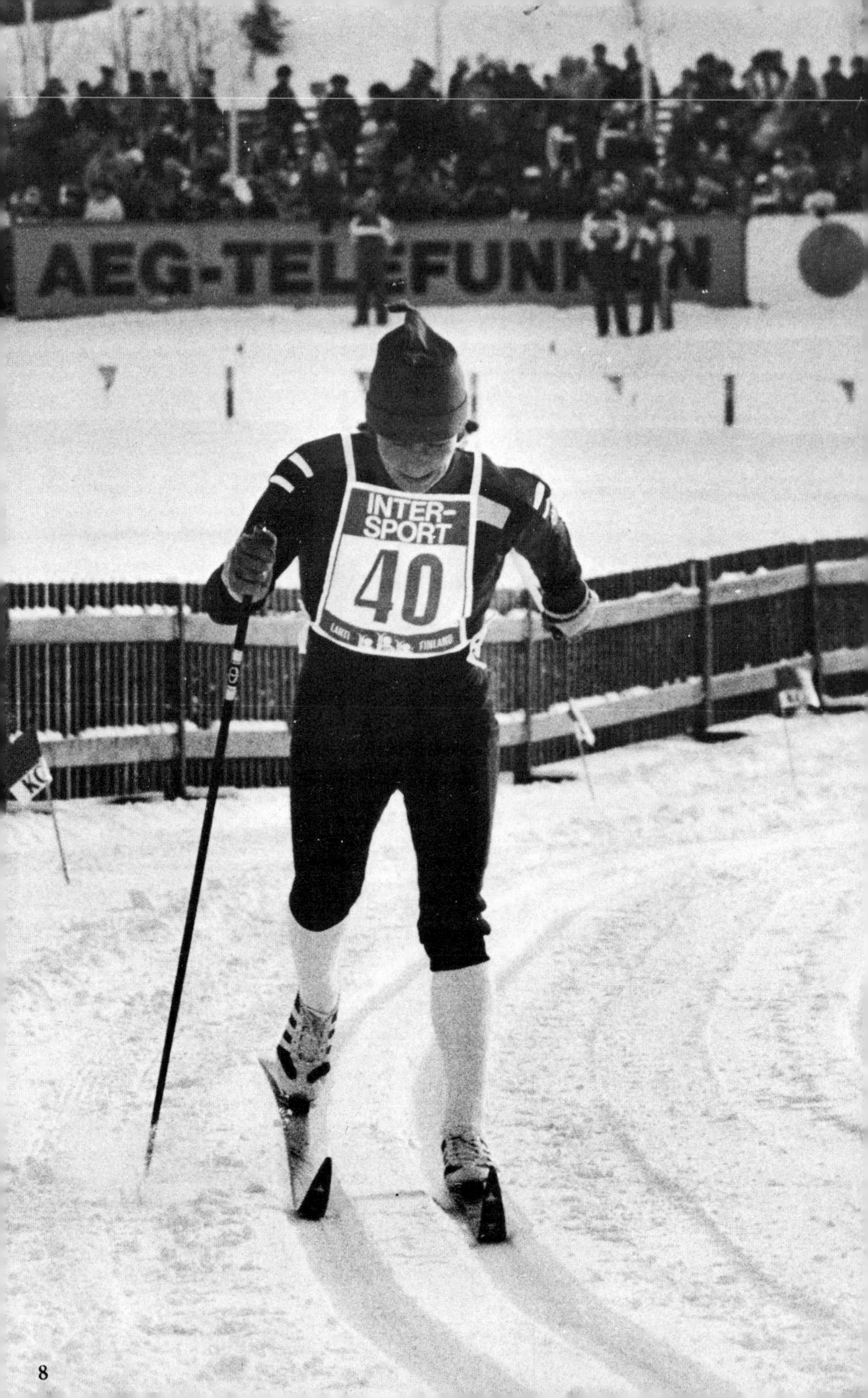
INTER-
SPORT
40

For some, like Galina Kulakova, left, the world's most bemedaled skier, cross country is racing. . .
In citizens' racing, such as the start of Sweden's *Vasaloppet,* above, you're not alone. . .

All in all, cross country is something to enjoy at your own pace, in your own style, for your own purpose. It can be as personal as the way you dress, as convivial as your friends and family, and as tranquil or challenging as you wish to make it. It can take you to a picnic or to a neighbor through woods or over mountains; or it can take you around race courses—all according to how fast and far you want to go. It's not limited by age, sex, athletic ability, or income.

In short, cross country skiing is what you want to make it, which may explain why cross country skiers now outnumber Alpine skiers worldwide.

Good technique is simply the way to ski naturally and efficiently.

Maybe you were all alone,  or maybe a parent was watching, when you stood up and shakily took your first step. In no time you toddled, then walked, then still later ran and jumped. You became a walker without ever knowing which foot your weight was on, without ever studying the theory of walking. Your skill as a born walker can make you a skilled cross country skier, because moving on cross country skis is similar to moving on foot.

The basic maneuver is the diagonal stride, a natural and reflexive movement that evolves directly from your normal walk. The other maneuvers shown in this chapter also have evolved from natural on-foot movements, and will follow easily once you can ski the diagonal stride. Together they make up cross country ski technique. Good technique is not complex or detailed, but simply the way of skiing naturally and effortlessly.

In cross country skiing, as in many other sports, the *racer's* technique is the most refined of all the sport's participants. Even so, that technique is the simplest and most natural. But good cross country ski technique *does not* require you to ski as fast or as far as a racer. Good technique simply

The basic diagonal stride on skis resembles your natural walk.

means that you use the same economy of movement that enables racers to cover distance fast and to ski without tiring. In fact, if you can walk, jog or run any distance, however long that may be, then you can ski at the same pace over the same distance. And you can do so with the same basic technique used by the racer.

This is why racers have been used to illustrate the technique shown in this book. Your arms and legs may not swing to the same extremes as the racer's, but the same principles will guide your skiing. Good technique can, in fact, be defined as the particular way of efficient movement that suits you best. With technique, you can enjoy skiing. Without it, you may struggle, plod, and waste energy.

You should be wary of exactly copying the sequences shown in this book, or from any other skier's style, because no two people, no matter how expert, ski exactly alike. Cross country skiing uses many natural walking movements, and most people have individual and clearly recognizable footsteps. So your strides will be your own. The technique sequences shown here should be guides, not goals.

**Glide Right:** The skier is gliding with weight on the right ski and neither pole is touching the snow.

**Swing:** Left leg and right arm swing forward in unison. The left pole has been planted in the snow.

**Together:** The kick on the weighted right ski starts as feet pass each other. Right pole forward swing and left pole pull continue.

## GETTING STARTED

If you are a beginner, the best place to start cross country skiing is at an area which has prepared tracks. Good tracks not only ease your initial learning, but also speed your progress by allowing you to ski as much as you wish. Cross country involves motion, and the more you move, the quicker you'll learn. If you don't have a track available, have friends who can ski help you make one. It need not be long, a few hundred yards will do.

Even with a good track, you'll probably fall at least once your first time on skis. So getting up may be your first technique hurdle. It's simple. Just crawl forward on your hands and knees, rise to your knees, then get up. Brush yourself off, and you're ready to start the strides.

## THE BASIC STRIDES

The basic cross country diagonal stride simply means that, like walking, you use the opposite arm and leg together. The arm plants the pole while the opposite leg pushes off or "kicks." You can learn the diagonal stride by starting with an ordinary walk on skis in a flat track. If you then lean more forward, as if into a wind, progressively increase your kick force, and swing your arms more, you'll have the correct diagonal stride. Just as in walking, the kick propels you forward. The pole helps in this maneuver; it supplies a tenth to one-quarter of your forward power.

If you are accustomed to Alpine skis, it may seem strange that your cross country skis can both grip and glide. The action of cross country ski bases on snow is very much like a stiff brush on a wet boat deck. If you

**Kick:** The right leg kicks backward, pushing the skier forward. The right arm is almost completely forward, and the left arm is pushing on its pole.

**Glide Left:** The opposite of Glide Right.

strapped brushes on your feet, you could kick off from one, and slide forward on the other. The basic principle applies to cross country skis. A ski will glide as long as it is in motion. Once gliding stops, it will stick until it is unweighted slightly so it can glide again.

The illustrations on this page show one complete pace of the diagonal stride. In the first two figures, the right leg and left arm are forward. In the last two figures, the left leg and right arm are forward. The diagonally-opposite limbs follow one another in their natural movements. Note that the head and shoulders are relaxed, and do not bob up and down or from side to side. Vertical or side-to-side motion does not push you forward.

In all cross country strides, the hand grip used on the poles is the key to relaxed, efficient arm movement. The correct grip is firm as angled poles are planted, and then allows the hand to open as the arm swings backwards. A fixed grip restricts movement and tires you quickly.

If you have trouble coordinating your arm and leg movements, practice skiing the diagonal stride without poles. Pole-less skiing also helps you

## Pole-less Diagonal Stride

| Together | Kick | Glide Left |
|---|---|---|

Diagonal without poles builds coordination and rhythm. Compare with last three photos of diagonal stride sequence.

learn the rhythm that smooths your diagonal stride. Get the feeling by striding out in a track, swinging your arms in unison with your legs. When you've got the feeling, use your poles again.

Your aim in the diagonal stride should be efficient glide, but don't overdo it. Keep your strides short at first; don't imitate better skiers' longer strides. Short strides, like those of your natural walk, are stable and comfortable. Longer strides will come naturally as you acquire rhythm and balance.

### Grip

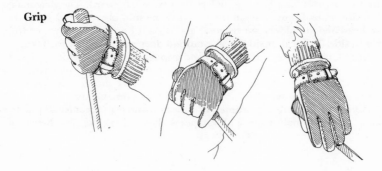

**Left to right:** When angled poles are planted in front, hand grip is firm but not tight. As the pole and arm pass the body, the grip loosens. When the arm is completely in back, grip is relaxed and the pole is held loosely between thumb and fingers.

## DOUBLE POLING

Double poling provides forward power: both arms work in unison, much as the natural movements you perform in jumping or diving. Double poling is used for variation in movement, or to pick up speed on the flat or on downhills.

As shown in the sequence on pages 16-17, the body bends at the waist and upper body weight on the poles provides forward thrust, much as if the skier were pumping an old-fashioned railroad handcar.

Double poling can be done with or without strides between successive pole thrusts. On the flat, or under resistant snow conditions, double poling takes more energy than the diagonal stride, so it cannot be maintained for long periods of time.

## DOUBLE POLE STRIDE

When a leg stride is added to double poling, it becomes the double pole stride. The double pole stride is mostly used as a variation to the diagonal stride, much as you might swing your arms or jog on a hike, just to relax. It can be done easily even with a rucksack on your back, as shown by the sequence illustrations on pages 16-17. The basic stride can be further modified by taking two complete kick-and-glide paces on alternate legs instead of one in between successive pole plantings. The arms keep the same movements, but there are two complete leg strides between the second and fifth pictures.

## CHANGING STRIDES

There is no set way to switch from the diagonal stride to double poling or vice versa; individual skiers use individual motions to maintain rhythm. One way of changing from the diagonal stride to double poling is to let one arm take a half pole movement. Another commonly used method is to skip a pole movement and hold the forward arm fixed until the opposing arm swings forward. Shifting from double poling to the diagonal stride is similar to the first three figures of the double-pole sequence except that only one arm is swung forward.

## Double Poling

**Pole Plant:** Double poling starts by setting both poles in the snow at arm's length ahead of the body.

**Sink:** As the body moves forward, the skier bends at the waist and knees, letting upper body weight sink over poles for forward thrust.

**Down:** Arms straighten to push on poles when the body is at its deepest bend.

## Double-Pole Stride

**Glide:** The skier glides on equally weighted skis, swinging arms forward as in the final phase of double poling.

**Kick:** One foot kicks down and back as the arms continue forward swing.

**Stretch:** The kick finishes, and the skier glides on one ski.

**Push:** The pole push finishes, and arms swing free in back of the body; grip on poles releases.

**Up:** Arms swing forward as body rises to an erect position.

**Glide:** Arms swing up for the next pole plant as the skier glides.

**Plant:** Poles are planted in the snow and the kicking legs starts to swing forward.

**Sink and Push:** As the kicking leg comes forward, the skier sinks over the poles and pushes, just as in double poling.

**Up and Glide:** The body rises to an erect position, and the skier glides.

## Star Turn

**Parallel:** Start with skis parallel.

**Step:** Here the skier steps to the left, angling the ski out and moving the left pole.

## Kick Turn

**Plant:** Here the skier will turn to the left. First the body twists to the left and the left pole is planted in the snow by the tails of the skis.

**Kick:** The left ski is kicked forward and up, and pivoted around its tail so its tip falls back.

## TURNING ON THE FLAT

### Turning at a Standstill
There are many ways to change direction on flat or gently sloping terrain. The simplest is to step your skis around, one at a time. This is the star

**Together:** The right foot and ski are now brought parallel to the left.

**Parallel:** The skier now repeats the steps to complete the full turn.

**Down:** The left ski is now on the snow, pointing in the new direction.

**Around:** The right ski is now brought around parallel to the left. Then the right arm and pole will move forward in the new direction.

turn, named for the pattern the skis make in the snow. The kick turn shown here puts your legs in a yoga-like position and requires more balance, but is quicker and can be done on hillsides. Attempt it only after you feel comfortable in the star turn.

### Skate Turn

**From Left to Right: Pole:** The skier starts a left turn with one double-pole movement, gliding on equally-weighted skis. **Skate out:** The left ski is unweighted and pointed to the left. **Push:** The right leg pushes the body onto the left ski. **Glide:** The right ski is brought parallel to the left. Arms continue to swing forward as the skier glides in the new direction.

## Turning in Motion

Whenever you change direction when walking, you simply take a step in the new direction. This is the basic maneuver in the *skate turn,* which is especially easy to learn if you have ever ice skated or roller skated.

The skate turn combines well with the rhythm of the diagonal stride or double poling, which is why it is usually begun and ended with a double poling movement. Properly done, the skate turn lets you maintain speed while changing direction. A good diagonal stride and a good skate turn are often considered the most important maneuvers in mastering cross country technique.

## GOING UP

In going uphill on skis, you use the same principles you might use in climbing a hill on foot. Just as you walk straight up a moderate hill, you can also ski straight up a hill using the *uphill diagonal stride,* which is nothing more than the ordinary diagonal stride with movements modified to suit the incline.

The uphill diagonal stride differs from the flat terrain diagonal stride in the same manner that walking uphill differs from walking on the flat. Because of the incline, arms and legs bend more and move less. Forward glide is shortened or disappears completely as the incline becomes steeper. The kick that provides forward power comes more from the toe than from the foot's rolling onto the toe. The body is in a more upright stance. These characteristics give the uphill diagonal stride its characteristic jogging appearance.

As the hill gets steeper, you may elect to zig-zag up, much as you might do in following the switchbacks of a foot trail on a hike. At each turn you'll maintain your diagonal rhythm by using the *tacking turn*, named for the tacking maneuver in sailing.

**From Left to Right: Step Right:** The left kick is nearly finished. Waist, knees and ankles are bent more than the corresponding position in the flat diagonal stride. **Together:** The right leg has started its kick. Note the on-toes left foot position. In the corresponding position of the flat diagonal stride the foot is flat on the ski. **Step Left:** The right leg is fully extended and the kick is finished; weight now transfers to the left ski. The right arm is pulling.

**Uphill Diagonal Stride**

## Herringbone

**Step Right:** The skis are opened in a V; the skier steps right using the natural walking diagonal rhythm.

**Step Left:** Weight is now on the right ski, and the left ski and right pole move uphill.

On still steeper hills, you may slide backwards using the uphill diagonal stride. Then it's time for the *herringbone*, a maneuver similar to what you do on foot to climb a steep hill: you walk duckfooted upwards, and your skis leave a herringbone pattern in the snow when you press the edges inward.

Finally, if the hill is too steep to herringbone, you may *sidestep*, which is walking uphill sideways with your skis across the fall line (the imaginary line that runs straight downhill) much as you might do on foot carrying furniture up stairs.

E

D

C

## Tacking

**A: Diagonal:** The tacking turn starts with the skier in the normal uphill diagonal stride.

B

**B: Step Left:** Here the skier starts a turn by stepping out the left ski. The left pole, planted in the snow, prevents sliding back downhill.

**C: Step Right:** The skier now brings the right ski and pole around together.

**D: Parallel:** The right ski is placed parallel to or pointing slightly inward towards the left ski.

A

**E: New Diagonal:** One step now puts the skier in the uphill diagonal stride in the new direction.

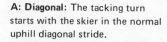

## Sidestep

**Together:** The right ski is now brought up next to the left. The right pole will move up next to the right ski to complete the step.

**Step:** The skier moves and plants the left pole and then the left ski uphill.

**Together:** The sidestep starts with skis parallel across the slope, both poles planted for stability.

## GOING DOWN

### Straight and Stop

Humans are bipeds by nature, and cross country skiing is a biped activity. Therefore it is physiologically correct to use the wide-track (skis apart) position in all downhill technique, which is the natural position of readiness and balance. The stances used in skiing downhill on cross country skis vary from the standing erect to the bending down in a high-speed egg position.

Whenever skiing downhill, the arms should be relaxed and low—as if you were holding the handlebars of a bicycle—and the poles should point backwards.

The *snowplow* is the easiest way to slow down or stop. It is named for the "V" position of the skis that plows up snow in the process of braking downhill speed.

## Downhill

**Stable:** Ankles, knees and hips are bent; the position is one of readiness. The bent knees absorb bumps, changes in slope, or transitions to patches of sticky snow.

**Crouch:** A high crouch or partial egg position, as often used is less than the more upright stance, yet stability is good.

**Egg:** The full egg position used in racing. The skier has a compact, streamlined position and the balance of the wide-track stance. However, the position is less stable than the partial egg and its compactness makes quick response difficult.

## Snowplow to Stop

**Brake:** Start a snowplow with knees and ankles bent and weight evenly on both skis. Press your heels outward until your skis are in the V position. Increase the snowplow's braking by spreading the ski tails further apart or by using a more knock-kneed position, which rolls the skis more on their inside edges and plows up more snow.

## Turning

The flat-terrain skate turn can be used on moderate slopes, while for steeper slopes you'll need other turns. Basic to all turns is that if one ski is weighted and pointed in a new direction, you will turn.

The simplest of all downhill turns is the *snowplow turn.* Turning is accomplished simply by leaning out over the left ski for a right turn, and the right ski for a left turn, as shown in the sequence.

The snowplow turn, like the basic snowplow, brakes your downhill speed. The *stem turn* allows you to turn more quickly while maintaining your speed. The stem turn starts by stemming out one ski, or pointing it in a new direction in what looks like half of a snowplow V. Weighting the ski causes you to turn. You should attempt the stem turn only after you have mastered the snowplow turn. As you gain proficiency, make the stem smaller, which speeds up the turn.

### Snowplow Turn

**Weight Left:** Here the skier starts a right turn by weighting the left ski, which is pointed to the right.

**Snowplow:** To start the turn, the skier brings both skis into the V snowplow position.

**Turn:** Weight is kept on the left ski by leaning out.

**Slide:** Skis are slid towards each other at the finish of the turn.

## Stem Turn

**Stem:** In a right turn, the uphill left ski is unweighted and "stemmed" or placed with its tail out and tip pointed towards the right ski in what looks like half of a snowplow V.

**Weight:** The body bends out and over the left ski and the right ski is unweighted. This transfer of weight to the left ski powers the turn.

**Parallel:** As the skis turn downhill through the fall line and in the new direction, the right ski is brought parallel to the left, completing the turn.

A still more advanced and faster turn is the *parallel turn*, which relies on weight shift and edging of skis to initiate and complete the turn. The parallel is Alpine skiing's most common and most polished turning maneuver; with practice it can be mastered on cross country skis.

## Parallel Turn

**Pole:** The skier is on a downhill traverse and prepares to turn left by planting the inside, right pole.

**Up:** The skier goes up to a more erect stance to unweight skis, allowing them to turn.

**Around:** The turn continues with the weight on the outside, left ski.

**Down:** The skis now point in the new direction, and the skier sinks down in the knees to complete the turn.

Skis, boots, bindings, and poles—the basic gear.

# CROSS COUNTRY EQUIPMENT CHARACTERISTICS

| Equipment Type | Skis | | Boots | | Bindings | | Poles | | Total weight: skis, boots, bindings and poles |
|---|---|---|---|---|---|---|---|---|---|
| | Waist Width | Typical 210 cm pair weight | Features | Typical size 42 (US 8½) pair weight | Type | Typical pair weight with heel-plates | Features | Typical 140 cm pair weight | |
| **Competition** | 44 mm (regulation minimum) | 1.1-1.4 kg | resembles track shoe, sole lip fits toe clip binding | 540 gr. | Toe clip | 80 gr. | Carbon-fiber shaft, small basket | 250 gr. | 1.97-2.27 kg. (4 lb 5 oz - 5 lb) |
| **Racing-Training** | 44-48 mm | 1.2-1.5 kg | resembles track shoe, fits Nordic Norm toe binding | 650 gr. | Nordic Norm toe piece | 140 gr. | Aluminum shaft | 350 gr. | 2.34-2.64 kg. (5 lb 2 oz - 5 lb 10 oz) |
| **Light Touring** | 46-52 mm | 1.5-2.0 kg | cut at ankle, fits Nordic Norm toe binding | 760 gr. | Nordic Norm toe piece | 155 gr. | Fiberglass shaft, small, round basket | 440 gr. | 2.86-3.36 kg. (6 lb 4 oz - 7 lb 6 oz) |
| **Touring** | 52-61 mm | 2.0-2.5 kg | cut above ankle, fits Nordic Norm bindings | 820 gr. | Toe piece / Cable | 210 gr. / 955 gr. | Fiberglass or tonkin shaft | 480 gr. | 3.51-4.01 kg. (7 lb 12 oz - 8 lb 13 oz) / 4.26-4.76 kg. (9 lb 6 oz - 10 lb 7 oz) |
| **Mountain** | 61 mm and over | 2.8 kg and over | resembles hiking boot | 1.7 kg. | Cable | 955 gr. | Fiberglass, aluminum or tonkin shaft, large basket | 520 gr. | 5.96 kg. and up (13 lb 2 oz and up) |

Selecting cross country equipment may, at first, seem more difficult than selecting other sports gear. This is because the spectrum of cross country equipment is broader than in any other sport.

At one end there's equipment for all-out speed; but it's expensive, delicate, needs good tracks, and requires greater skill to use. Then there's the workhorse equipment: sturdy, reliable and capable of any terrain—but heavier and cumbersome for all but the most arduous skiing. Either at these extremes or somewhere in between you'll find equipment to fit your skiing needs. The best equipment for you is not always the lightest, newest or most advanced-technology gear. It's the equipment that best suits your skiing ability and habits.

## EQUIPMENT TYPES MATCH USE

Cross country ski equipment varies in characteristics and construction according to intended use. The major categories, compared in the Table on page 30 are *ski mountaineering, touring, light touring,* and *racing.*

*Ski mountaineering* equipment is, as the name implies, for skiing remote terrain which, if traversed in summer, would classify as mountaineering. *Touring* equipment is preferred by many wilderness skiers and backpackers. The broader skis, higher boots, and sturdier bindings also feel more stable to many beginning skiers. Touring skis have profiles that makes them easy to turn in loose or untracked snow. *Light touring* equipment is now the most popular for all-around cross country skiing, especially in well-skied areas or wherever tracks are available. *Racing* equipment now comes in two types: *racing-training* for racers and expert light-touring skiers who ski prepared tracks, and *competition,* for racing on well-prepared tracks.

When buying equipment, stay within one category, and then select according to your needs and budget. If you are in doubt, or simply just want to try cross country skiing, then rent your equipment: "ski and see" is a good philosophy that may save you money in the long run.

## SKIS

Skis are best described by the characteristics that determine their skiing performance: measurements, weight, and flex (or stiffness of their various parts).

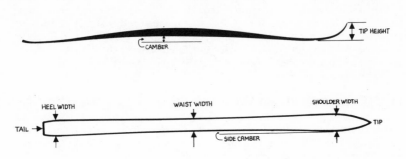

The anatomy of a ski.

Ski length, usually the only measurement imprinted on skis, should be about 30cm. (14 inches) longer than body height for best performance. All ski manufacturers state lengths in centimeters, but not all measure lengths in the same way. The most common ways of measuring ski length are *material length,* along the base of the ski from tip to tail, and *chord length,* a direct line from tip to tail. These different methods of measurement result in skis with identical imprinted lengths sometimes being unequal in length.

Ski widths are almost always stated for the waist, the middle and narrowest part of a ski. In general, the wider a ski, the more base area it puts on the snow, and therefore the less it will sink in and the more stable it will feel during skiing. This is why the different use categories of ski are classified primarily according to waist width: 44 to 48 mm for racing skis, 46 to 52 mm for light touring skis, 52 to 61 mm for touring skis, and over 61 mm for mountaineering skis. The difference between the waist width and the shoulder and tail widths, where a ski is widest, is called side camber, or side cut. Side cut helps a ski to track, or run straight on snow. Also, side cut is one of the properties that helps a ski, when banked on snow, to follow a curved path.

Flex, a ski's stiffness, refers to the way the various parts give and rebound in skiing. A good cross country ski should have a soft tip that "flows" easily over bumps, and be progressively stiffer back towards its waist to properly carry skier weight. Stiffness should decrease towards the

Typical cross country skis, from left to right: mountain ski with aluminum edges (Fischer, Austria), touring ski (Splitkein, Norway), light touring ski (Epoke, Norway), racing ski (Skilom, Norway), competition ski (Karhu, Finland); all skis are fiberglass.

tail so the ski will flex evenly and not chatter off of bumps, while still being harder than the tip to support skier weight and aid turning.

Camber is the arch in the middle of a ski above its tip and tail. Camber and overall stiffness determine the force necessary to flatten a ski on the snow, as needed for grip. The downward force a skier can apply, such as during the kick in the diagonal stride, depends on body weight and skiing ability. Beginners, for instance, generally transfer no more than two-thirds of their body weight onto a ski while racers, who have rapid, emphatic kicks, may apply downward forces equal to more than three times body weight. This means that, for a given body weight, beginners should select "softer" cambers than more proficient skiers, while racers should select "harder" (stiffer) cambers. Skis with excessively hard cambers relative to a skier's weight and proficiency will run on their tips and tails; their mid sections will contact the snow poorly or not at all, which will cause frequent slip instead of grip. Skis that are too soft will run on their mid sections, which reduces glide and tracking ability.

## Waxable or Waxless?

Cross-country skis must both grip and glide on snow. Therefore, cross-country ski bases are classed either as *waxable*, to take waxes that grip and glide, or *waxless*, with a surface that grips and glides.

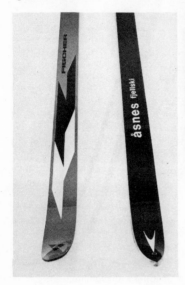

Typical ski bases, from left to right: waxable, and hair strip, pattern, composite material.

Fiberglass vs. wood: typical fiberglass (left) and wood (right) mountain skis have almost identical dimensions.

Waxable bases are potentially the best performers, because wax can be changed and modified to match ski bases to various snow conditions. This is why waxable skis are used almost exclusively in racing. But waxing can be difficult, especially when snow is in the transition between wet and dry just at freezing, 32°F, or when snow conditions change during a tour. For these conditions, waxless bases can outperform waxable bases, which is why they are popular with recreational skiers, and why several models of waxless skis have been successfully used in racing in transition snow conditions.

The major advantage of waxless bases is their convenience. If, for instance, you suddenly decide to go cross-country skiing, waxless skis are ready to go. But modern, wide-range cross-country ski waxes are so simple to use that waxing is no longer as complex as it once was. Therefore, if you ski changing snows only infrequently, the choice between waxable and waxless skis reduces to whether or not you are willing to learn waxing to achieve the performance it provides.

**Waxable Skis:** There are two main types of waxable ski bases: wood bases on wood skis and plastic bases on some wood and all synthetic skis. Wood bases have their traditional advantage of being the original waxless base: at sub-freezing temperatures, they can grip and glide with little or no wax. But they have the disadvantage that they must be prepared with tar compounds to retain their waterproofing and hold wax. Unprepared, wood bases absorb water, which can then freeze and damage the base surface, weakening the ski. Wet or iced bases hold wax poorly or not at all. Plastic bases are waterproof and, when correctly waxed, can outperform wood bases, but they have the disadvantage that they must be waxed to grip and glide: without wax they only glide.

**Waxless Skis**: There are three main types of waxless ski base, according to the nature of the surface irregularity that provides grip on the snow: *hair, pattern* and *composite material.*

Modern hair bases are descendents of the hair-based "kicker" skis of a century ago. Hair is laid in the plastic base in strips or small rectangles, with the nap angled backwards for grip. Natural or synthetic mohair and Fibre-tran are used. Hair strip bases have the advantage that they can easily be replaced when worn. But, like any garment of hair, they can absorb water and freeze. And when frozen, they cease to function properly. Silicone waterproofing sprays are available to hinder hair strip icing.

Pattern bases have irregularities with profiles resembling overlapping shingles that glide forward but grip in the backwards direction. The scale, step, diamond, crown, oval, circle and other patterns moulded, stamped, or otherwise machined into the plastic bases are either *positive,* where the pattern is embossed, or raised above the base, or *negative,* where the pattern is below the base surface. Some negative patterns are more durable and more easily repaired than positive patterns. But, in general, performance depends more on base quality and overall ski structure than the method of manufacturing the waxless base irregularities. Pattern bases seldom freeze. But they wear, which degrades grip with ski age. Some patterns emit a squealing sound as they glide.

Composite material bases function on a principle analogous to that of studded tires: small, backward-slanting particles grip, while the plastic in which they are imbedded glides. The chief advantage of composite bases is that the waxless action is a property of the base material and thus is retained as the base wears.

All waxless ski bases have some resistance to forward glide. In high-performance models, skimakers now compensate for waxless base drag by limiting the waxless section to the center of the arch of the ski's camber, which usually is in contact with the underlying snow only when the ski is fully weighted, as during the kick that provides forward power in the diagonal stride. Tips and tails of these skis have smooth bases which may be waxed with paraffin waxes for glide. Several wax makers offer special glide waxes or aerosol sprays for just this purpose.

### Wood Skis—The Traditional Nordic Choice

Wood skis are built from many laminations, a construction method developed and patented in the early 1930's in Norway and the USA. The lamination technique produces skis that are stronger, lighter, and more resistant to warping than those made of solid wood.

Laminated skis are built using the "sandwich" method. Several horizontal layers, each composed of many laminations, are bonded together in a press that gives the ski its final shape. The top and bottom layers, which must carry most of the stresses to which the ski is subjected, contain the strongest woods. The center layers, which act more as fillers to give the ski its shape, generally use lighter, weaker woods.

In general, the more laminations and/or the greater use of stronger woods, the stronger and better quality the ski. The stronger woods, such as hickory, are more expensive, so production costs go up with the increased numbers of lamination. Higher quality wood skis are therefore higher priced.

Wood skis may have wood, compressed wood, or plastic bases. Traditional waxable wood bases, such as hickory or birch, perform well on most snow conditions with little and sometimes almost no wax, but must be prepared well to hold wax. Compressed, impregnated beech ply bases, such as *Permagli* and *Neswood*, need no preparation and are durable, but don't hold wax as well and are heavier than hickory or birch. Waxable plastic bases are light and need little preparation, but must be waxed to perform. All waxless bases on wood skis are plastic.

Wood ski making is an expensive and somewhat wasteful woodworking process. Approximately one-third of the wood used in production goes into finished skis; the rest is rejected in inspection or discarded as chips and sawdust from the woodworking machines. This, combined with the relatively large amount of hand work required, means that wood skis, like other hand-crafted products, have become more expensive in recent years.


## Fiberglass skis

First introduced in quantity in 1974, fiberglass cross country skis dominated the market within three years. Fiberglass skis are generally stronger and, in some types, faster than their wood counterparts. However, for comparable quality, they may be more expensive because they use more expensive materials. But their manufacture is more easily automated than that of wood skis, so volume production can lower fiberglass ski prices.

By definition, a fiberglass ski is one in which the structural material, without which the ski would literally fall apart in use, is fiberglass. The fiberglass used is actually a cloth-like weave of thin filaments of glass, all encased in a plastic, usually epoxy. For this reason fiberglass skis are sometimes called "Epoxy" or FRP—"Fiberglass Reinforced Plastic" skis.

Two basic types of fiberglass ski construction are used: sandwich and box. The sandwich construction is similar to that of wood skis: the upper and lower structural layers are laminated onto a central core. Box construction consists of a layer of structural material fully encasing a core. Some skis are hybrids, using a combination of these two processes. Both methods have advantages, but neither can be said to be superior. Ski performance and quality depend more on factory capability, material quality, and production skill and accuracy than on basic ski construction.

Construction of typical wood and fiberglass skis.

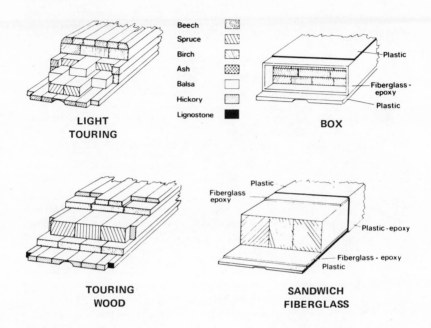

Beech
Spruce
Birch
Ash
Balsa
Hickory
Lignostone

**LIGHT TOURING**

**BOX**

Plastic
Fiberglass - epoxy
Plastic

**TOURING WOOD**

**SANDWICH FIBERGLASS**

Plastic
Fiberglass epoxy
Plastic - epoxy
Fiberglass - epoxy
Plastic

### Cores—a profusion of types

There are almost as many core constructions as there are brands of fiberglass skis. This is because core properties must compromise among the desired goals of high strength, light weight, resistance to warp, ease in production, good bond to structural materials, and reasonable price. Wood, foam plastic, aluminum honeycomb and mixes of these are used in cores. Wood and foam plastic are the most commonly used.

*Wood* has the advantages of being available in a wide range of properties, strong in shear (difficult to break across the grain), strong in bonding, and easily worked in traditional ski-making methods. Wood's disadvantages are that it can warp if not carefully treated during manufacture, and that some of the woods used in ski making are becoming scarce and expensive. There are two ways of making a wood core: lamination and mortoise joining. Both can use a single or several types of woods.

*Foam plastic* cores were first used in lightweight racing skis. The most common core foams, polyurethane and acrylic (short for polymethacrylimide) are available in a wide range of properties. Polyurethane has the additional production advantage that it can be formed integrally in a mold with the ski in an injection process. Plastic foams are light, easy to shape and bond and can be less expensive than wood. However, foam has low shear strength and doesn't hold binding screws. When a foam core is used, a ski must also have a special layer in the foot area for holding binding screws.

As for basic ski constructions, manufacturer skill and material quality are more important than the particular core material or production method used.

### Other parts

The tops, bases and sides of fiberglass skis are made of various types of plastic, depending on location in the ski. Most top sheets are made of ABS, a tradename for Acrylonitile Butadiene Styrene, although some skis have polyethylene top sheets. The best bases are now made of polyethylene, which is also known under its Swiss tradename P-Tex, or polypropylene. A few bases are made of ABS or its related compounds. Ski sides may be epoxy coated, or made from a plastic such as ABS.

### Choose Edges According to Use

For most cross country skiing, the edges of plastic bases and the lignostone edges on the majority of wood bases are adequate. But for wilderness skiing or ski mountaineering on hardpack snow and ice, these edges don't have enough bite. Result: they wear quickly. For such conditions, partial or full-length aluminum or steel edges are advisable. Aluminum edges are lighter, while steel edges are more durable and can be sharpened as they wear.

## BOOTS

Typical boots and bindings, left to right: touring, light touring and racing.

Cross country boots are as varied as the corresponding footwear for off-snow activities. Cross country racing boots are cut low, below the ankle, have leather or nylon uppers, and generally resemble track shoes. Light touring boots are sturdier. They are usually cut at the ankle, like men's shoes, and most models have leather uppers. Touring boots resemble hiking boots. They are usually cut above the ankle, and most models have double lacing or a double tongue for waterproofing. Ski mountaineering boots resemble sturdy hiking boots. They may be single or double layered, and many models have lug soles.

Up until the later 1960's, most cross country ski boot makers used the Norwegian welt construction, in which boot uppers are sewn to laminated leather or leather-rubber sandwich soles. Now, however, most boots have moulded soles, to which the uppers are attached by injecting, vulcanizing or bonding. The Norwegian welt construction is now used only for some light racing boots and for heavier touring and mountain boots. In the bonded construction, finished rubber or plastic soles are cemented to boot uppers. In vulcanizing, which involves rubber, or injecting (which involves plastic), the soles are formed and fused in a mould onto the uppers. As for ski making, each of these sole-to-upper attachment methods has its advantages, but none of them can be said to always be superior. The durability of the bond and sole quality depends more on the skill of the bootmaker than on the particular process used.

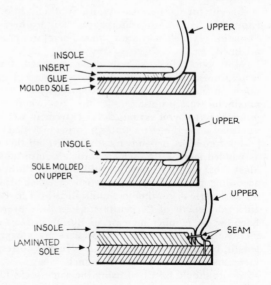

Three basic boot constructions.

## Inside and Outside. . .

Cross country boots may be unlined or lined. Boots lined with natural or synthetic fleece are warmer, but take longer to dry and retain foot odor longer than unlined boots. For weekend skiers, these differences are minor, but if you ski often, unlined boots with extra socks for insulation are best.

Boots are classified primarily as being either leather or synthetic. Leather boots have leather uppers, and only minor parts such as tongues and collars are sometimes made of other materials. Most boots are of leather, because leather can "breathe" yet still be waterproof.

Tanned cowhide is the most common leather used for ski boots. The hide of an adult animal is too thick for boot uppers, so it is split into thinner sheets. The outside, or top sheet, is called *top grain*, regarded as best for boot uppers as its tough surface and natural oiliness resists moisture. All other layers are called *split leather*. Split leathers have rough surfaces that resemble suede, but can also be coated with plastic to resemble top grain. Some boots have "rough out" uppers, which may be either reversed top grain or roughened split. Rough out leathers don't show scratches or scuffs, but are often less waterproof than top grain or plastic-coated split uppers.

Except for light-weave nylons, synthetic boot uppers are usually less expensive and more waterproof than leather, although they do not "breathe" as well and are colder. Therefore, most synthetic boot uppers are lined.

Most boots have sewn-in bellows tongues, which provide adequate waterproofing for most needs. Most tongues of this type, even on leather boots, are made of padded synthetic textile materials for flexibility and maximum waterproofing under the laces where snow often collects when you ski. But if you ski mostly in extremely wet or deep unbroken snow, you may need the extra waterproofing provided by a double-tongue boot.

Boot comfort depends mostly on fit, but there are other features, such as padded snow cuffs, which form a comfortable seal around the ankle. Most cross country boots are still made in Europe and are sized primarily according to the European system in which sizes are simply the boot's inside length in centimeters multiplied by 1.5. For example, a boot with an inside length of 26 centimeters (a little over 10 inches) is a size 39. Each whole number increase in European sizes corresponds to a length increase of 2/3 centimeter. U.S. sizes are not as conveniently related to length, but whole number increases in size correspond to an inside length increase of about one-third of an inch.

Boots should be fitted using the same socks that you will use in skiing. Allow ample toe clearance for foot movement in the various ski strides. A good test for clearance is to push your foot forward in a loosely-laced boot until your toes touch; you should then be able to get two fingers down in the boot behind your heel.

# BINDINGS

Cross country skiing requires that the heel be free to lift off the ski. Bindings must allow maximum forward foot freedom while holding the heel laterally for good ski control. Cross country bindings differ from release-type Alpine ski bindings, which must overcome the dangers of rigidly attaching the foot to the ski with a stiff and inflexible boot-binding combination. Every movement of an Alpine ski is transferred to the firmly-attached foot and leg: every small ski twist is a corresponding leg twist. The greater flexibility of cross country boots and the heel freedom of boots in bindings makes the connection between skis and feet loose and flexible. This, combined with the light weight of cross country equipment makes cross country skiing inherently safer than Alpine skiing.

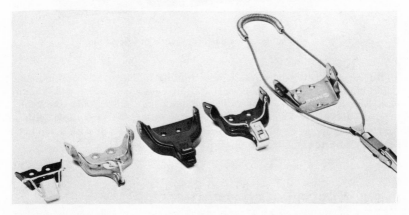

Typical bindings, left to right: Racing Norm competition, metal light touring, plastic light touring, metal touring, cable-type touring/mountaineering.

Several models of cross country bindings are available; all share the common principle that a boot is attached only at the very tip of the sole. This attachment allows complete freedom of movement: a pair of well broken-in cross country boots fastened in bindings are only a little stiffer than tennis shoes.

There are two general types of cross country bindings: toe bindings, which clamp the front part of the boot sole into the binding, and cable bindings, in which a heel cable presses the boot toe forward into the toe piece.

Toe bindings, which are by far the most common, are made of metal or plastic and differ from one another only in the way the boot sole is guided and clamped. The two major types are the pin binding, in which a bail presses the boot sole down against pins projecting upwards from the toepiece base plate, and the clamp binding, in which clamps engage the boot sole.

Cross country boots in bindings are as flexible as tennis or jogging shoes.

All racing, light touring and most touring bindings are toe bindings. Cable bindings are used for heavier touring equipment and for mountain skis. The toepieces of most cable bindings are similar; only the cable mechanisms differ. There are two types of cable: the heel cable with a front or rear spring to provide tension, and the heel strap with a ratchet-loaded clamp to provide tension. Both are adjustable.

## THE BOOT-BINDING CONNECTION

Almost all boot soles and bindings are now standardized to fit one another. Three systems are now used. Oldest and most prevalent is the *Nordic Norm*, which specifies binding and boot sole side angles and three standard widths, 71mm, 75 mm and 79 mm, as measured at the pine holes. Most common is the 75 mm width; most light-touring boots in all but the largest sizes come only in this width. The soles on Nordic Norm boots are at least 12 mm (about ½ inch) thick.

Newer are the *Norm 38* and *Racing Norm 50 mm* boot-binding systems, originally developed for racing. In both systems, a forward extension, or "snout" on the boot sole engages the binding. The soles on these boots are thin, about 7 mm (about ¼ inch) thick, and usually made of a hard plastic, which can be slippery underfoot when walking. The advantages of these systems are lightweight, and right-left interchangeability of boots in bindings. The major disadvantage is that the thinner boot soles are usually colder on the feet than the thicker Nordic Norm soles. A recent hybrid that solves this problem is the *Touring Norm 50 mm* system, in which boots have Racing Norm 50 mm profiles and shape, but thicker, 12 mm, soles. This type of boot has proven sturdy enough for expedition skiing.

The three boot-binding systems, left to right: Nordic Norm, Racing Norm, Norm 38.

Bindings made according to these standard systems all mount with three screws, one forward, and two rear. The center of the forward binding mounting screw is located 47 mm (about 1½ in.) ahead of the centerline of the rear two screws, which are spaced 32 mm (heavier Nordic Norm bindings) or 26 mm (most Nordic Norm bindings, all Racing Norm, Touring Norm and Norm 38 bindings) from each other. These standard screw spacings ease binding mounting and replacement.

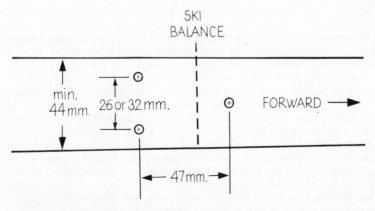

Standard screw spacings for toe bindings.

Bindings should be mounted so the front edge of the boot uppers, corresponding to a line through the outer pins of a pin binding, is just over the ski balance point. This placement lets the ski tip drop downward when the ski is lifted in the cross country strides so it will follow and hold the snow surface. Racers prefer to mount their bindings about 1.5 cm (9/16 in.) further back for still better tip follow and slightly better glide on fiberglass skis.

Typical heel plates: metal teeth (left) bite into rubber boot heel, wedge (right) fits groove in boot heel. Both act to hold weighted boot heel on ski.

# POLES

Cross country ski poles are classified chiefly by their shaft material: tonkin, fiberglass, carbon fiber, or metal.

**Tonkin,** the traditional natural shaft material, is named for its major source, the Gulf of Tonkin. Tonkin is relatively strong, light, lively, and inexpensive, which explains why it has long been the leading material for pole shafts. However, the processing of raw tonkin into shafts suitable for poles requires many manual operations. Labor costs have recently made quality tonkin shafts as expensive as some mass-produced synthetic shafts. Tonkin shafts have the disadvantage that they can absorb moisture and crack in storage. However, minor damage to tonkin shafts can be repaired by taping.

**Fiberglass** shafts are made from cylindrical or tapered, extruded tubing, with the fiberglass filaments running longitudinally along the tube, in spirals around the tube, or both longitudinally and in spirals, all encased in plastic, usually polyester or epoxy. Tubing with longitudinal fiberglass encased in polyester is the least expensive and the weakest. When damaged by impact, such as in a skiing fall, these shafts may collapse completely. Tubing with spiral or longitudinal-and-spiral fiberglass filaments encased in epoxy is far stronger, but also more expensive.

**Carbon fiber** shafts are usually tapered tubes with carbon fibers running longitudinally, anchored by spiral fiberglass, all encased in epoxy. The chief advantage of carbon fiber shafts is that they are far lighter than all other shafts. They can also be made stiffer, an advantage for competition poles. Carbon fiber shafts are expensive compared to other materials, and therefore are used only on competition poles.

**Metal** shafts are made of tapered or cylindrical steel or aluminum alloy tubing. A wide variety of metal shaft qualities and prices are available, all according to the quality of the material used.

Pole baskets come in a variety of shapes and sizes. Most common are the traditional round baskets, which ride well on top of loose snow. Basket diameters vary from about 9 cm. (3½ in.) on light touring poles intended for use on prepared tracks, up to about 15 cm (6 in.) on ski mountaineering poles intended for use in powder snow. There are also a variety of assymetrical racing baskets, designed primarily to ease pole plant on machine prepared and packed racing tracks.

Pole grips are made of plastic, cork, leather or synthetic leather. One-piece molded plastic grips are the least expensive, while cork and leather grips are warmer, more comfortable, and absorb perspiration.

Pole tips are set at an angle to shafts to ease pole plant and withdrawal in the arm movements of cross country. Most tips are made of hardened steel alloy, of a type similar to that used for the studs on studded snow tires.

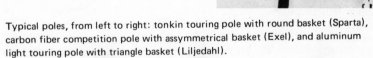

Straps differ: left - nylon web strap
curls up in handle (Exel). Right - leather
strap adjusts with buckle (Liljedahl).

Typical poles, from left to right: tonkin touring pole with round basket (Sparta), carbon fiber competition pole with assymmetrical basket (Exel), and aluminum light touring pole with triangle basket (Liljedahl).

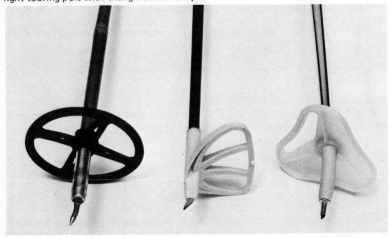

Poles are classified according to use, but in categories slightly different from those for skis, boots and bindings.

**Competition poles** have tapered metal or carbon fiber shafts with maximum diameters of 15 mm (9/16 in.) or less. Their grips are made from leather or cork, and wrist straps are adjustable. Baskets are assymmetrical, and usually angled to the shafts. Shafts are stiffer than those of other pole types, for maximum poling power in machine-packed competition tracks.

**Racing and light-touring poles** have metal, fiberglass or tonkin shafts. Shaft diameters range up to 16 mm (5/8 in.), and may be tapered or cylindrical, except for tonkin which is cylindrical only. Grips are made of leather, cork or plastic, and wrist straps are adjustable. Most baskets are round, up to 9.8 cm (3 - 7/8 in.) diameter, but some models have assymmetrical baskets. Shafts are stiffer than those of touring poles, but not as stiff as competition poles.

**Touring and mountain poles** have cylindrical metal, fiberglass or tonkin shafts up to 17 mm (11/16 in.) diameter. Grips are are made of leather, cork or plastic, and wrist straps may be fixed or adjustable. Baskets are round, up to 15 cm (6 in.) in diameter. Shafts are more flexible than racing and light touring shafts, which gives them an easier feel in heavy snow.

## ABOUT LENGTH

There is no one fixed rule for ski and pole length. As a guideline, select skis about 30 cm. (one foot) longer than your height, and poles about 35 cm. (one foot, two inches) shorter than your height. For most adults, this is equivalent to a ski reaching to the palm of an upraised arm, and a pole fitting comfortably under an outstretched arm, with the skier standing, wearing ski boots or low-heeled street shoes. Children may select skis and poles slightly longer, to grow into. Some shorter, more powerfully-built skiers prefer longer skis, to obtain ski stiffnesses that suit.

Ski and ski pole lengths should match skier height.

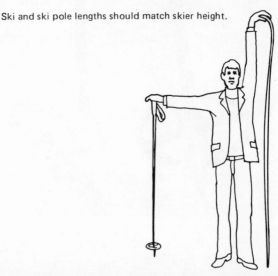

Cross country waxes both grip and glide.

A well-waxed cross country ski lets you stride on the flat and ski up hills without slipping backwards, and slide downhill without sticking. The wax both grips and glides.

A waxed ski behaves this way because small microscopic irregularities of the snow surface penetrate the wax just enough to allow a good grip when a ski is weighted, yet allow a moving ski to glide. Once gliding stops, the ski must be unweighted to start it gliding again. In scientific language, this is explained by saying that the coefficient of static (non-moving) friction is far greater than the coefficient of dynamic (moving) friction.

From this ideal, a ski may be improperly waxed in two directions: "too hard" or "too soft." If the wax is too hard for the snow surface, the snow will hardly penetrate at all, and the ski will only glide: it will not stand firm when weighted. This is the ideal for Alpine skiing and jumping: to present a surface that slides well on the snow involved. If, on the other hand, the wax used is too soft, the snow particles can penetrate too far into the wax. The ski only grips and doesn't glide. The snow particles may even remain in the wax, which makes the skis collect snow and ice up.

A weighted ski grips.　　　So you can kick.　　　But a ski in motion glides on a microscopic water layer.

The microscopic snow particles' own atmosphere also plays an important role. Snow particles lubricated with a water layer will slide over a waxed surface more readily than if they are "dry." The secret of waxing is to determine the type of snow involved, and then properly apply the right wax.

The difference between standstill and moving friction is what makes cross country wax work. Even some unwaxed skis may both grip and glide under certain conditions. But if they were waxed properly, they would both grip and glide better: waxing increases the difference between static and dynamic friction. Correct waxing makes skis perform better and protects them against wear and moisture. A good skier wears wax, not skis.

### THE BASICS
The art of waxing covers everything you intentionally apply to the bases of your skis: wax, base preparation, base wax, or cleaners.

*Wax:* There are different waxes to match different snow conditions. *Hard waxes* are for new or slightly settled "dry" snow below freezing. *Klister-waxes* are for wetter new or settled snow. Hard waxes and klister-waxes come in small metal foil, plastic or cardboard containers. *Klisters,* thick fluids that come in toothpaste-style tubes, or in sprays, are for still wetter or more settled snow. *Glide waxes* are used for increasing glide on polyethylene ski bases, and come in either containers like hard waxes or in wax blocks. With few exceptions, waxes are colored, with different colors for the various snow conditions.

The number of waxes you'll need depends on how involved you wish to get in waxing. If you prefer simplicity, select *wide-range waxing,* where two or three waxes cover most recreational skiing needs. If you are a beginner, wide-range waxing is a good start to learning the art. If you want top performance, select *full-range waxing,* in which you'll use the full lines of eight to 15 waxes offered by major makers. If you're a racer or skilled light touring skier interested in speed on fiberglass skis, then you'll probably opt for *high-performance waxing,* a variety of full-range waxing.

*Base preparation* includes the impregnating tars that are applied to wood bases for protection and waterproofing, and the paraffins that are applied to polyethylene bases for speed.

*Base waxes* (also known as "binders") increase wax adhesion. There are two types, hard base wax, and base klister.

*Cleaners* are liquid or spray solvents used to remove wax.

### Putting It On
Waxing indoors is best. It's not only more comfortable, but the room temperature makes wax easier to apply and smooth out. Always start with clean, prepared, dry skis. Wax won't stick to dirt, road film or water. If your skis need cleaning, see "Taking It Off." The way wax is applied depends on wax type.

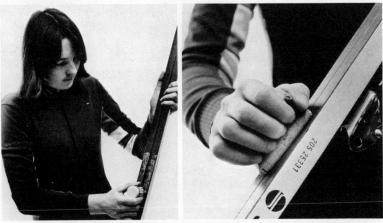

Crayon on hard wax in short strokes.     Rub out hard wax or klister-wax with a cork.

Apply tube klister in strips.

Spread klister out with a paddle.

Hard wax or klister are best removed with a scraper.

*Hard waxes:* Start by exposing some wax, either by peeling off part of the container or by pushing the wax up, depending on the brand. Then crayon the wax on in short, rapid strokes, covering the base evenly. Then rub the wax smooth with a waxing cork. Several thin layers are better than a single, thick layer. More layers give better grip; fewer layers better glide.

*Klister waxes:* Start as with hard waxes, but put on in short strokes or by dabbing against the base. Don't rub, or the wax will come off in gobs that are difficult to smooth out. Rub the wax smooth with a waxing cork or, if your hands are clean and dry, with the palm of your hand.

*Klisters:* Squeeze out tube klister in an even strip on each side of the tracking groove; then smooth it out with the applicator usually packed with each tube. Apply spray klister evenly over the base area. Klister hardens when cold, so if you must wax outdoors, try to keep your klister warm—either by carrying it in an inside shirt pocket or by gently heating the tube (*not* a spray can) in the flame of a waxing torch.

### Taking It Off
Like waxing, cleaning is best done indoors. Always clean skis before applying new wax or preparing bases. Klister hardens on skis in storage within a few days to a few weeks, depending on storage room temperatures. So if you are a weekend skier, it's best to clean klister off your skis before putting them away for the week.

Start cleaning by scraping off all old wax with a ski scraper. A plastic scraper is best for this job, as it will not damage bases if your hand slips.

After you've removed as much as possible with a scraper, finish the job by heating the bases gently with a waxing torch and then wiping off melted wax with a rag or cleaning tissue, or apply wax-removing solvent to the bases and wipe clean with a tissue or rag. *Caution:* Use cleaning fluids only in well-ventilated areas, as they often are flammable or toxic, or both.

### WIDE-RANGE WAXING
In wide-range waxing, two or three waxes are all you'll need to ski in most snow conditions. The performance of wide-range waxes doesn't equal that of the better wax-to-snow match available by using more wax types, as in full-range waxing. But for simplicity wide-range waxing is best.

Typical wide-range waxes.

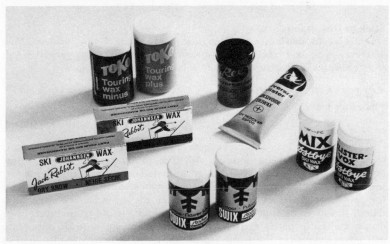

**Check Snow First**

Determine wax type and application by checking the snow. Snow may be either "dry," usually below $0°C$ ($32°F$), or "wet," above $0°C$ ($32°F$). Thermometers are not always reliable for snow temperatures, especially if they are mounted high above ground level or are in the sun. So always double check snow wetness by squeezing a handful in a gloved hand. If the snow blows away easily when you open your hand, it's dry. If it forms lumps or a snowball, it's wet.

**Read and Apply**

After you've checked the snow, check the manufacturer's directions and select the wax to match snow conditions. Read the directions on the can or tube before applying: different makes of wax require slightly different applications for best results. Then apply the wax. For very cold conditions, $-3°C$ ($26°F$) and below, rub "dry" wax out smooth with a waxing cork. For warmer conditions still below freezing, leave the wax a bit rougher. The principle is the same for "wet" waxes applied above freezing: the higher the temperature, the rougher the wax layer applied.

**Change When Needed**

When in doubt, test ski your wax. But don't judge it before you've skied about 500 yards, the distance wax needs to run in.

If your skis slip backwards, you've waxed too cold. Correct by adding a rougher wax layer in the middle of the ski base, starting a few inches ahead of the binding and extending back to just under the heel of your boot. If you still slip in cold conditions, add "wet" wax in small amounts for grip. If your skis drag or collect snow, smooth out the wax more with a waxing cork. If the problem persists, you've probably waxed too wet, and you must then scrape off the wet wax and apply dry wax.

**Stick to One Brand**

One secret to mastering waxing is to pick a brand that you can buy wherever you ski and learn to use it well. Knowing one brand's characteristics further simplifies and speeds up your waxing.

**FULL-RANGE WAXING**

Full-range waxing of wood and recreational fiberglass skis matches wax to snow more exactly than wide-range waxing does. Therefore, snow conditions must be more exactly classified.

Falling snow flakes and crystals have many sharp points and edges. As soon as they hit the ground, they start changing. At very low temperatures, snow crystals are hard and resist crushing: this is powder snow. If the temperature stays low, newly-fallen snow may stay powdery for days or even weeks. If it's warmer when the snow falls or after it has fallen, it will settle quicker and may even melt. If the temperature then drops, melted or partly melted snow can refreeze. Subsequent remeltings and refreezings alter the snow still more. Snow is therefore classified as

Full-range waxes from four major wax makers listed in the table.

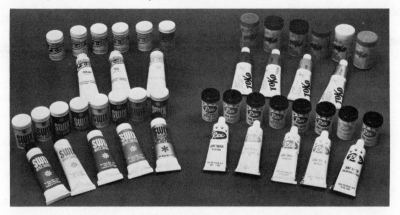

Don't cool by placing skis in the snow, which may cause icing. New wax needs about 500 yards of skiing to "run in" and grip and glide well.

falling and new, settled, or changed (metamorphosed). In each of these cases it can be dry, wet, or in the transition range between dry and wet. These standard classifications are used in the waxing table.

As in wide-range waxing, the simplest guide to judging snow type is to squeeze a handful of snow in a gloved hand. If the snow doesn't clump at all and you can blow it out of your hand, it's dry. If it just barely clumps and you can blow some of it away, it's transition. If it clumps into a snowball, it's wet. Temperature, if correct, is also a good guide. The temperatures listed in the table are approximate, and are measured in the upper snow layer for temperatures below freezing, and as still air temperature in the shade for temperatures above freezing. Use an outside wall thermometer only as an approximate waxing aid. Better yet, carry and use a waxing thermometer.

The waxing table lists the products of six major wax makers that offer a full line. It is intended only as a guide and is not exact for all the products listed. Always follow manufacturers' directions on containers before waxing.

Wax the entire running surface of the ski. Be especially careful in waxing the bow of the ski's camber, the part of the ski where the difference in weighting between glide and grip is greatest. The direction wax is applied or smoothed out makes no difference at all. For any particular wax, total surface roughness makes some difference: the more polished its surface, the more glide. Ironing on a wax tends to give it more glide. After ironing, always polish wax with a cork.

For abrasive snow conditions, wax durability may be increased by first applying base or "binder" wax. Base hard wax and base klister are applied in the same manner as final hard wax and klister. Base wax should always be applied thin and smoothed out well.

Always let newly waxed skis cool to outside temperature before skiing.

## WAX TABLE

| | Snow Type and Characteristics | Temperatures usually are in the range | | EX-ELIT Sweden |
|---|---|---|---|---|
| | | °C | °F | |
| **FALLING AND NEW SNOW** | Very Cold (light powder) | −12° and below | 10° and below | Cold Special (Black) |
| | Extremely Dry (falling powder) | −8° to −15° | 5° to 18° | Cold Special (Black) |
| | Very Dry (powdery: blows easily) | −3° to −10° | 14° to 27° | Green |
| | Dry (blows with difficulty) | −1° to −5° | 23° to 30° | Blue |
| | Borderline Dry (barely blows) | 0° to −1° | 30° to 32° | Blue |
| | Transition (clumps in gloved hand) | 0° to −1° | 32° to 34° | Violet/Red |
| | Mushy (rolling snowballs dig in) | 0° to +3° | 32° to 37° | Yellow |
| | Wet (hand soaking wet after squeezing) | +2° to +6° | 35° to 42° | Tö Kristall klister |
| **SETTLED SNOW** | Very Cold (light powder) | −12° and below | 10° and below | Cold Special (Black) |
| | Very Dry (small crystals will blow) | −8° to −15° | 5° to 18° | Green |
| | Dry (small crystals will form snowballs) | −1° to −10° | 14° to 30° | Blue |
| | Transition (large crystals, corns, or clumps) | −1° to +1° | 30° to 34° | Violet/Red |
| | Mushy (hand wet after squeezing) | 0° to +3° | 32° to 37° | Red/ Tö Kristall klister |
| | Wet (slushy) | +2° to +6° | 35° to 42° | Tö Kristall klister |
| **ALTERED SNOW** | "Skare"−Dry, Hard, Ice, Crust, etc. | −5° and below | 21° and below | Skar Kristall klister |
| | Crusty but Softer to Mushy and Wet | −6° to +1° | 22° to 34° | Skar Kristall & Tö Kristall klisters mixed |
| | Wet Slush | 0° to +6° | 32° to 42° | Tö med tjära klister |

*NOTE: Klisters are in tubes, and all other waxes are in cans. Listing under a manufacturer is only a guide. READ THE MANUFACTURER'S DIRECTIONS ON THE CAN OR TUBE BEFORE YOU WAX.*

| FALL-LINE U.S.A. | REX Finland | RODE Italy | SWIX Norway | TOKO Switzerland |
|---|---|---|---|---|
| Light Green | Arctic/ Turquoise | Alaska Racing | Polar | Green Special |
| Green | Light Green | Light Green | Special Green | Green Special |
| Green | Green | Green | Green | Green |
| Blue | Blue | Blue | Blue | Blue |
| Blue | Blue Special | Blue Super | Blue Extra | Violet |
| Purple | Violet | Violet | Red Special | Red |
| Yellow | Yellow | Yellow | Yellow | Yellow |
| Red | Red klister | Red Special Klister | Yellow klister | Yellow/ Red klister |
| Light Green | Turquoise | Alaska Racing/ Light Green | Polar | Green Special |
| Green | Light Green/ Green | Green | Special Green/Green | Green Special/ Green |
| Blue | Blue | Blue | Blue/ Extra Blue | Blue |
| Purple | Violet/ Violet klister | Violet/ Violet Klister | Red Special | Violet |
| Red/ Purple Klister | Red/ Red klister | Red/ Red klister | Red/ Violet | Yellow |
| Red Klister | Red klister | Red klister | Violet | Red klister/ Violet klister |
| Blue Klister | Blue klister | Blue klister Red klister/ | Blue klister | Blue klister |
| Purple Klister | Silver klister | Violet klister | Violet klister | Violet klister |
| Red Klister | Special OI, OB klisters | Black klister | Red klister | Silver klister |

## TARRING WOOD BASES

Wood ski bases must periodically be prepared to seal out water and moisture and to aid wax adhesion. Wood absorbs water easily; wet skis can freeze, and wax doesn't stick to ice.

The compounds used to prepare wood bases contain tar and resemble common creosote wood preservative. There are two types: air-dry preparation, which is either sprayed or brushed on, and warm-on tars. Bases should be prepared whenever base wood shows through. For most recreational skiers, once at the *end* of each season, to avoid absorbing moisture during storage, is enough.

Applying tar,

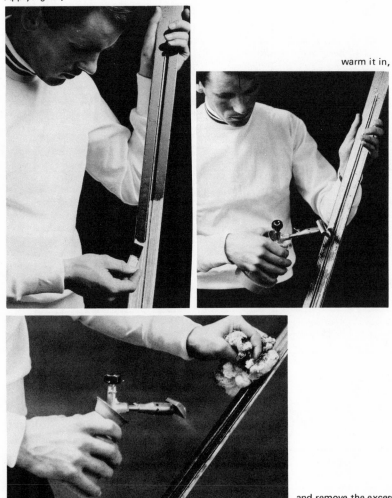

warm it in,

and remove the excess.

Start by scraping the base flat, clean and smooth with a carpenter's scraper. Finish with fine sandpaper or steel wool. Some wood skis are treated at the factory and therefore need no preparation until they have been used awhile. If in doubt, discuss the factory base-coating type with your dealer.

*Air-dry impregnation* is brushed or sprayed over the entire base. Most air-dry compounds dry in two to eight hours.

*Warm-in tars* protect bases better and give better wax adhesion. First, brush the fluid tar compound over the entire base, and then warm it slightly with a waxing torch until it bubbles and smokes slightly. Then remove the excess with a rag or cleaning tissue. Keep the waxing torch moving continually so it doesn't burn any part of the base. The result should be a dry base, about the color of dark milk chocolate.

Sometimes warming tar into bases increases ski camber. You can restore original camber by strapping the skis together, gently heating their tops with a torch, and letting them stand strapped together for a day.

## High-Performance Waxing

High-performance waxing for competition, citizens' racing and high-speed skiing on fiberglass and carbon-fiber skis differs from the traditional full-range waxing of wood skis and recreational fiberglass skis for several reasons.

First, the fiberglass, carbon-fiber and similar constructions used in high performance skis produce camber and stiffness distributions that differ from those of wood and recreational fiberglass skis. The midsections of the bases have little or no contact with the underlying snow when both skis are equally weighted, as in downhill skiing or in gliding after double poling. However, during the kick, with the weight all on one ski, the middle

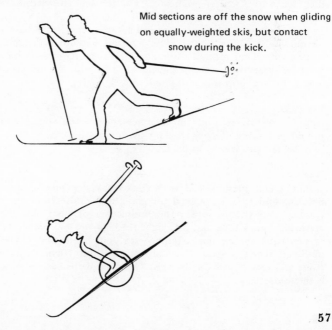

Mid sections are off the snow when gliding on equally-weighted skis, but contact snow during the kick.

of the base is pressed against the snow. Therefore, the middle of the base is more dominant in grip, and the tip and tail more important in glide than the corresponding areas of a wood ski, or a recreational fiberglass ski base. This is why tips and tails are waxed for glide, while midsections are waxed for grip in high-performance waxing.

Finally, thermoplastic bases, especially polyethylene, are most durable and glide best when well prepared with paraffin wax.

## Base Preparation

Most high-performance skis have polyethylene bases, sometimes labeled by tradenames such as P-Tex or Fastex. New polyethylene bases should always be prepared, and then retreated whenever they appear dry. Use Alpine paraffin ski wax, or better yet, special cross country base-preparation paraffin.

Start base preparation with skis horizontal, bases up. Melt paraffin wax onto the skis with a heated waxing iron or electric iron; $100^{\circ}$C to $130^{\circ}$C ($212^{\circ}$F to $266^{\circ}$ F) is the ideal iron temperature, which just causes the melting wax to smoke lightly. Hold the corner of the iron just above the ski base, and let the wax drip down to leave strips of melted wax on both sides of the tracking groove. Then smooth out the wax with an iron.

Let the skis cool at room temperature until the wax has hardened, which takes 15 to 30 minutes. Then scrape the wax on the base to a thin, smooth layer using a steel carpenter's scraper when preparing new skis. With used skis, a rectangular plastic scraper, which will not damage the base should your hand slip, is best. Scrape until the wax seems to have been almost completely removed; only the wax that has penetrated the base remains. Remove excess wax from the tracking groove with a soft object shaped to fit the groove, such as the tail of a cheap ball-point pen or the corner of a klister applicator. For the less fussy, thumbnails can be used.

Some manufacturers recommend treating the entire base while others recommend treating only the tip and tail, excluding the midsection that will be waxed for grip. If the midsection is prepared with paraffin wax, it must be scraped even more thoroughly than the tip and tail, since this is where the final grip wax is applied.

## Base Wax

Apply base wax in the same manner and for the same conditions as for full-range waxing of recreational skis, but apply only in the middle of the base, where grip wax is applied.

## Waxing

Waxing techniques, as well as choice of wax, depends on snow conditions. Ski tips and tails are waxed for glide, and midsections for grip. Before waxing, you should locate the midsection of your skis. Hold the skis vertically, bases together, and sight through the gap made by the cambers as you squeeze the skis together with your hands placed just behind the bindings. When the gap closes down to about 70cm (2½ feet) mark its front and rear points on the skis. The part of the base between the marks is the midsection.

Start base preparation by melting paraffin wax onto base

then smooth it out with a heated waxing iron.

After it has cooled, scrape it to a thin, smooth layer.

Remove excess wax from tracking groove with a suitably shaped, soft object.

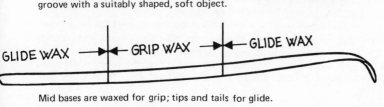

GLIDE WAX — GRIP WAX — GLIDE WAX

Mid bases are waxed for grip; tips and tails for glide.

Sqeeze skis together to locate mid section.

*Grip wax* is applied in the midsection of the base, over a length determined by snow conditions and hardness of ski camber. To increase grip, increase the length waxed for grip, more forward than back, because grip wax on ski tails behind midsections will drag and reduce glide.

*Glide wax* is applied in the same manner as base-preparation paraffin. Most major wax makers offer a range of glide waxes keyed to temperature and snow type or to their line of grip waxes. For dry, cold snow, -8° to -10°C (16°F to 19°F) and below, cross country wax for extreme cold conditions can be used instead of glide wax. The advantage is that the glide attained equals that of glide-waxed skis, while the grip wax applied can be thinner and shorter than were the skis glide waxed.

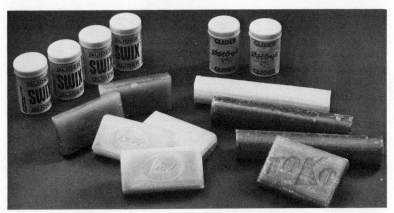

Most major wax makers offer glide waxes keyed to their grip waxes.

*Wet snow:* Freshly base-prepared skis need no further tip and tail waxing. Apply wet snow klister to the middle 60cm to 80cm (24-32 in.) of the base, preferably in two layers with the first is warmed in. For used skis, a new coat of glide wax may be needed on tips and tails.

*Transition conditions, moist snow:* When snow and air temperatures are around freezing, snow properties change very quickly. Therefore there are no fixed rules for the length of grip wax to be applied. Generally, klister applied for grip should cover about 70cm (28in.) of the base, while hard grip wax should cover about 90-100cm (35-40 in.) of the base. Glide wax tips and tails.

*Ice klister conditions:* For grip and durability, apply blue or other ice klister for a length of about 75-100cm (30-40 in.). Apply in two or more layers, preferably warming the first in. To increase grip, add extra layers in the middle of the section waxed. Grip may be further increased by dabbing in softer klister, such as violet, over a short section of the area waxed with blue klister. For temperatures of -5°C (23°F) and colder, apply base wax before klister to increase its durability. Glide wax tips and tails.

*Dry new snow and fine-grained snow:* Apply hard grip wax to a completely clean base, preferably in two or more layers, with the first is warmed in. Polish each layer with a waxing cork. The grip wax length

Final wax the center of the base. Here klister is shown being applied. Note the glide-waxed section.

Smooth out final wax with a warm waxing iron. Do not heat subsequent layers of different waxes, if applied.

depends on snow conditions, ski camber and stiffness, and skier technique, and can be as long as 90 to 150cm (35 to 60 in.). Tips and tails should be glide waxed with a type suiting the prevailing temperatures or, for colder conditions, waxed with a grip wax for extreme cold.

## Waxing Aids

*Ski scrapers and waxing corks* are great helps. They do a faster, more effective, less damaging job than tools not designed for the purpose. Many types are available, both separate and as combined scraper-corks. Corks, as the name implies, were once made only of natural cork. Synthetic corks are now more common. Most synthetic corks are made of expanded plastics, which are hard plastic foams.

*Wiping tissue,* such as Fiberlene, is virtually lint-free and therefore ideal for wiping when cleaning or tarring skis. It's also handy for polishing hard waxes.

*Pocket waxing thermometers* aid judging snow conditions.

*Waxing irons* are small, light, and available in several types. The best are

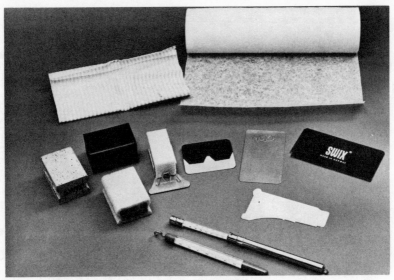
Typical waxing aids: corks, scrapers, thermometers, tissue.

solid rectangular aluminum blocks fixed to insulating handles, intended for heating with waxing torches. Electric waxing irons are also available; some skiers simply use a small electric travel iron.

*Waxing torches* are used for warming in base preparations, removing old wax, drying wet skis before waxing, and heating waxing irons. Almost all waxing torches now available are fueled either by propane or butane gas. For instance, Primus torch heads are available to fit U.S. disposable propane bottles and, with adapters, refillable propane tanks, while the Gaz torch heads fit the company's line of disposable butane cartridges. The propane cylinders are heavier than the lightweight butane cartridges for the same amount of gas, but have the advantage that propane burns well down to -30°C (-22°F) while butane "freezes" at -1°C (31°F). The choice between the two types depends on use and fuel availability. For a touring torch, the choice is between a heavier torch that is reliable, and a lighter torch that sometimes must be warmed inside clothing or by hand in subfreezing weather.

Whenever using a torch outdoors, use your body as a wind shield. In subfreezing weather, allow butane torches to run a few minutes after they are lit, and keep the cartridge tank and valve stem as vertical as possible while in use.

*Special wax-dissolving hand cleaners* and most mechanic's waterless hand cleaners will remove wax from hands and clothing. Ordinary vaseline is a good solvent for klisters. These types of cleaners should not be used on skis, as they are slightly greasy and will make subsequent waxing difficult.

*Wax kits,* as supplied by major wax makers, have compartments that hold all waxing needs. Most racers and expert skiers consider them a must.

*Waxing horses* are collapsable waxing stands that firmly clamp skis, bases up, at a convenient height. They are ideal for racers or coaches who often prepare and wax many pairs of skis.

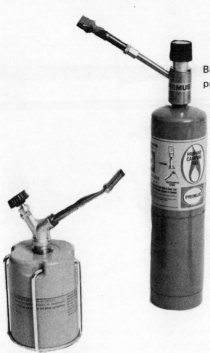

Butane waxing torches in foreground, propane waxing torch in background.

Collapsable waxing horses are convenient if you prepare and wax many pairs of skis.

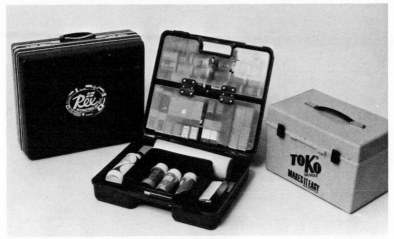

Wax kits hold all waxing needs.

## SKI CARE

### Maintenance

Clean waxed skis always before they are to stand unused for several days or more. Clean the bases with a scraper and heat, or wax-removing solvent and wiping. Clean tops occasionally with solvent.

Skis otherwise need little care. Scratches in bases, tops and sides need not be repaired if they don't go through to underlying layers or slow the ski. Base scratches in polyethylene are best repaired using base-repair "candles" that are lighted to drip molten plastic into the scratch. Scratches on ski sides and tops are best repaired with two-component epoxy filler. Scrape repair joints smooth with the surrounding surfaces, especially on bases.

Check binding screws periodically and tighten if necessary. Racers should always check binding screws before starting a race. Most bindings are now mounted with Pozi-Drive screws, usually size No. 3. These screws require special drivers. In a pinch, you can use a Phillips screw driver, but don't use it often as its tip flute angles and depths differ from Pozi-Drive and repeated use may damage screws.

### Storing Skis

Clean skis before storage. Carefully remove all wax, as wax hardens with time, and can be difficult to remove later.

Don't store wood skis with base wood showing. Always prepare wood bases before storing skis: it prevents moisture absorption.

Repair deep scratches and other damage before storage.

Fiberglass, carbon fiber, or high-quality, well-prepared wood skis will retain their camber and stiffness in storage, regardless of whether they stand, lie, or are strapped together at tip and tail. Store skis in a dry place where temperatures do not exceed 40°C (104°F) for long periods.

# CLOTHING AND ACCESSORIES

In cross country, the word is light.

### Clothing—Light is Right

The main goal of cross country clothing is to keep you warm by conserving your body heat. But clothing must also allow freedom of movement and be light; it should insulate, but not constrain or burden your skiing movements.

Cross country skiing can be enjoyed in a wide variety of clothing. All that's required are garments that insulate, are moderately windproof and water-repellant, and do not restrict arm or leg motions. But cross country is best done in clothing specifically designed for the activity. As is the rule for equipment, the best clothing is that which best suits the type of skiing you do. This is primarily because your need for insulation depends on weather conditions and how actively you ski.

In cold weather, most body heat loss is through the skin. The lower the temperature or the more cold air that comes in contact with the skin, the greater the loss. This is why both low temperatures and wind cool the body. Body heat loss also increases if the clothing next to the skin is wet, because water, whether it be from your own perspiration or from snow or rain, is an excellent heat conductor. Clothing should insulate and protect you against wind and water, as required by the weather where you ski.

Several light clothing layers insulate better than a single heavy layer. From left to right: transport underwear forms the first layer; knee socks and a sweater the middle layer; and a stretch nylon two-piece touring suit the outer layer.

As you ski, your muscles burn calories, coverting them into physical motion and heat. This heat, which corresponds to three-quarters or more of the calories you burn, helps you keep warm in cold weather. Heat may be more efficiently trapped with more insulation, or more can be produced by more muscle activity. Therefore there are two basic ways to stay warm: insulate with more clothing or keep moving. The more motion, the less clothing required, and vice versa.

The amount of clothing you need depends on how fast you burn calories. The average sedentary adult burns about 1800 calories a day, or about 1.2 calories per minute. The average recreational cross country skier burns nine calories per minute, while cross country ski racers burn from 25 to 35 calories per minute. This means that recreational cross country skiers, who burn 7.5 times as many calories as persons standing still, need far less clothing to stay warm. Racers, who burn three times as many calories as recreational skiers, need still less clothing for the same warmth. This is why you must select clothing that suits your type of skiing.

## Layers are Best

Actually, clothing fibers do not insulate: they conduct heat away from the body. It's the trapped air in and between clothing layers that insulates. The more trapped air, the greater the insulation. This means that several light layers of clothing are better than a single thick layer, because each layer traps air. Also, multiple layers allow you to take off or put on garments to suit activity and weather conditions. If you're warm when skiing, you may get cold if you stop to look at the scenery or take a lunch break. That's the time to put on another layer, such as a nylon windshell or another sweater.

There are three types of clothing layers, inner, middle and outer. The *inner layer*, such as long underwear, functions mainly to keep the skin dry. Two basic types are available. The *transport* type, such as "fishnet" or Super Underwear, allows perspiration to pass through and eventually evaporate rather than remaining next to the skin. The *absorption* type, like wool, which absorbs as much as 35% of its own weight in water before it feels wet, is a traditional. Although wool is the traditional standby, many active skiers perspire too rapidly to take advantage of wool garments next to their skin. These skiers, or persons whose skin is irritated by wool, should select the transport type of underwear, which can always be worn under wool. Always avoid cotton next to the skin when dressing for cold weather; as cotton retains moisture and chills you quickly.

The *middle layers* insulate: the more insulation needed, the more layers should be worn. Typical for middle layers on the upper body are turtle-neck sweaters, shirts, or vests. Legs, from the knees down, seldom need middle layer insulation: knee socks are adequate for most cross country skiing except in the most extreme cold weather conditions.

The *outer layers* both protect against the weather and, being visible, set your clothing style. Functionally they should be windproof or water-repellent as needed, and be permeable to internal moisture. Two and one-piece suits that end at the knee offer the freedom of movement needed in cross country, unlike slacks or stretch pants which hinder leg and knee movement. Caps and gloves or mittens complete the outer layer.

The types of garments in the three layers depend on the type of skiing done. *Racing* clothing is suitable only for continuous fast skiing. Middle layers are usually eliminated, and racers dress in transport-type underwear topped by knee socks and lightweight one-piece knit nylon racing suits that allow full body freedom and maximum permeability for escape of body moisture. Racing suits with windproof woven nylon fronts are available for racing in severe winds. When warming up before a race or skiing slowly, racers wear two-piece warmup suits, which have full zipper legs so pants can be put on or taken off while on skis. Light touring skiers often carry racing warmup suits as extra clothing.

*Light touring* clothing is suitable for skiing at most cross country areas. The outer layers, one- and two-piece stretch nylon or poplin suits, resemble racing clothing but are made of heavier fabrics for warmth. Two-piece suits allow the greatest flexibility in dressing and are now available with two different types of knickers, waist-high and bib height. The traditional belted or elastic waist knickers are light, but in skiing tops and bottoms of this type of suit can separate, exposing underlying layers or skin. Bib knickers and one-piece suits avoid this problem. One-piece suits are lightest, but present problems in answering the calls of nature out on the trail. Most light touring skiers prefer one or two middle layers, usually a turtleneck and a shirt. Underwear can be the transport type, or wool; many skiers combine layers by wearing wool over transport underwear.

*Touring and ski mountaineering* clothing for off-track wilderness skiing depends on the terrain, weather conditions, and length of tour. Durability, warmth, water-repellency and windproofing are of greater importance than minimum weight or style. Most wilderness skiers opt for poplin outer garments for protection against wind and snow, and carry several types of middle-layer garments to suit the temperature extremes encountered.

Cross country clothing should fit fairly snugly, without hindering movement. But it shouldn't flap in the breeze, or fold and bind. Garments should overlap to prevent gaps that expose skin. Mittens and gloves, for instance, should be long enough to extend under blouse or parka sleeves, and knickers should overlap knee socks.

Warm-up suits fit over other clothing

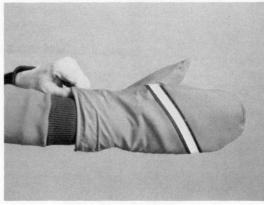

Racing and light touring gloves have perforated backs to let moisture escape.
Mittens are best for cold weather touring.

## Hands, Head and Feet

Caps and gloves or mittens are as necessary in cross country as in any other cold weather activity. An otherwise fully-clad skier may lose as much as a fifth of his total body heat through his hands and another fifth through the scalp if improperly clothed.

There are racing and light touring gloves with perforated backs to maximize ventilation while providing insulation. But mittens are best for most recreational skiing at temperatures below freezing. For extreme cold, multi-layer mittens, such as wool inner mitts topped by poplin shells, are best. Wool mittens alone are a poor choice, as pole straps can quickly wear holes in wool.

Knitted wool caps are almost the universal choice of cross country skiers. Racers usually wear lighter caps, while recreational skiers may use heavier double-layer caps that extend down to cover the ears. Parkas with hoods provide further head protection in extreme weather conditions.

Lightweight racing and light touring boots may not be warm enough in extremely cold weather and can get wet in slushy snow. Rubber or plastic-reinforced stretch nylon pullover socks are available to add insulation and water repellency.

## Packs, Pulks and Other Things

Most parka pockets are roomy, but they have their limits. Packs are better for most tours. A good cross country ski pack must fit the back well so as not to disturb body balance. It must allow full arm movement, and place the carried weight close in to the body where it will not upset balance on downhill runs or turns. Frame rucksacks or internal-frame ski packs are best for cross country. Large backpacking packboards and packframes, ideal for touring on foot, have loaded centers of weight that are too high for skiing. Small frameless packs are ideal for shorter day tours, but are cumbersome when loaded with the equipment necessary for extended tours. Small waist packs are ideal for day tours; some models are large enough to carry a camera, waxing aids, wax and a lunch.

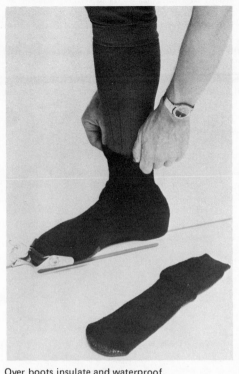

A well-fitting rucksack carries
the load close to the body.

Over boots insulate and waterproof.

Pulks can carry provisions or be
over-snow baby carriages.

71

*Pulks,* small multi-purpose wood or fiberglass sleds drawn by a skier or a dog are ideal for loads too cumbersome or heavy for packs. Some pulks come with a waterproof cover and a drawstring closure, a windscreen, and a reclining seat for use as an over-snow baby carriage. Smaller pulks will carry loads of about 45kg (100 pounds), while larger models, intended for use with dog teams, will carry 100 kg (220 pounds) or more.

If wood skis break, they usually break at the tip, so a *spare ski tip* is a must for longer tours. Several models are available. The most common is simply a plastic sleeve that fits over the broken ski tip. Also indispensable for longer tours is a *snow spade,* which can be used for a variety of purposes from emergency shelter building to collecting snow to boil for drinking water.

Unless there's a full moon, skiing at night can be a bit tricky without a flashlight. But it's difficult to hold and guide a flashlight while skiing. A *headlamp* solves this problem. The most common types have a separate headlamp and battery pack to minimize weight on your head.

*Track-setting sleds* make speedy work of preparing groomed trails. There are many models, most of which are designed to be towed behind a snowmobile. They are a must for race tracks and are now used by most major cross country ski areas.

A lightweight aluminum spade has many uses.

A spare tip is a must for long tours with wood skis.

Headlamps are a must for night skiing.

Track setters are now used for race courses and in many cross country ski areas.

Cross country ski racing is unique among athletic events (Bill Koch in 1976 Winter Olympic 30 km race, where he won a Silver Medal).

Cross country ski racing is unique among athletic events. Its shortest international distance, 5 kilometers (about 3 miles) is one of the long-distance events in track. Its longest international distance is 50km (31 miles), longer than the runner's marathon. Citizens' races may be even longer, up to 90km (56 miles). No other athletic event requires the use of so many body muscles over such long periods of time; physiological tests show cross country ski racers to be the best conditioned of all athletes.

The competition in cross country racing is keen. Often mere seconds separate the medal winners from each other, even in races that last up to several hours. In the 1978 FIS Nordic World Ski Championships' men's 15 km race, two seconds separated the silver and gold medal winners, in a race that lasted 49 minutes, equivalent to losing a mile track meet race by a yard. In the 50 km event, the medalists all timed within 70 seconds of

Any age is right for cross country racing.

each other, in a race that lasted almost three hours. Unlike track meet races, cross country ski racers start separately, at half minute intervals. Rivals seldom see each other during a race. Few know where seconds lost go. Any seemingly minor waste motion in a stride is repeated thousands of times in a race. Waxing can be tricky. A split second's hesitation in a high-speed turn could cause catching a tip, costing speed, energy and time. A little extra gulp at a feeding station can lose seconds, as can passing a feeding station and suffering a slow down later. A pole tip can slip on a steep hill, causing at best a break in rhythm, at worst a fall. Alone, the racer relies on coaches and teammates along the track for timing to gauge progress against that of rivals. Times and placings shouted to a racer can be misunderstood, or, even worse, incorrect, causing misjudgment of a vital part of the race. The possibilities are endless. More than any other event, cross country ski racing requires the racer to plan, judge, and compete alone.

**The Way Racers Ski**
Like many other competitive sports, cross country ski racing is now a far cry from what it was a decade or two ago. Thanks mostly to more scientific training, today's racers are, on the average, younger and ski faster than

their predecessors. Modern equipment and racing tracks have also aided this development. Even the past ten years have seen a jump in equipment performance and track quality. Modern fiberglass skis are far faster than their wood forerunners; boots and bindings are lighter and allow more foot freedom. Poles are lighter and more accurately apply arm power to forward motion. Waxing has become almost a science, and lightweight clothing leaves little to chance. Machine prepared to exacting specifications, the tracks of modern international race courses are made for all-out speed.

In terms of technique alone, modern racing is no break with the past, but rather a matured version of strides that developed through the years. Racing is a continuous, rhythmic movement; there is no substitute for seeing it done first-hand. A book or an illustration is not alive: it can tell you but it cannot show you how to race. Only the highlights of racing will be given here; with these in mind, *go watch a race.*

The sequence illustrations in the chapter on Technique are a guide to racing technique. The basic differences between good racing technique and good recreational technique are that racing movements are more rapid; racers' limbs stretch out more with speed. Racers also use more of the high-speed maneuvers that require more energy to maintain. For example, today's racers double pole more than recreational skiers, and even more than the racers of just a few years ago. This is because modern competition skis, waxed for glide speed on tips and tails, are fastest when equally weighted and gliding. Therefore they are proportionately stronger in their arms and upper bodies than recreational skiers or racers of the pre-fiberglass competition ski era (before 1974).

Even so, there's no one correct modern racing technique, as no two skiers ski exactly alike. Good racing technique is rather a framework of physiologically correct movements on which skilled racers build their own skiing style.

Major among the basic principles is that of a relaxed, forward-leaning, neutral body position. Seen in motion, the body seems to stay in one position as arms and legs swing forward and back as the skier glides ahead. Moving the body in any direction other than forward wastes energy.

Second, forward movements are active, but they are not jerks or kicks. The energy put into forward arm and leg movements depends on the speed and length of a race. Good racers have an active forward arm and leg drive on all steep uphills and, to a lesser extent, on gradual uphills and flats. They have the condition to maintain this drive throughout the length of their events. Like runners, they can sprint by speeding up their forward movements.

Third, body joints follow or flow with limb movements. Hips are not fixed, but rotate about a central axis. A backward-swinging leg draws its hip along. A forward-rotating hip swings its leg forward. Shoulders follow arm movements, extending their reach forward and back.

Finally, all arm and leg movements are as parallel as possible to the track. Movements that do not result in forward speed are unwanted, no matter how small they may be. Every movement the body makes uses energy. Wasted movement is wasted energy, and energy waste lowers speed.

These economies of movement make up the framework of good racing

Juha Mieto of Finland (skiing the 1976 Winter Olympic 15 km) shows the neutral body position with arm and leg movements parallel to the track. Note general body forward drive.

technique. Above all, endurance is the key to successful racing, as technique and endurance depend on one another. If your technique is good, you last longer. If your endurance is poor, you tire quickly and your technique worsens, which just tires you more rapidly. So maintaining technique in a race depends on physical training.

## Training—The Essential
Training is any physical activity that improves or maintains physical ability. It need not be strenuous, hard, or unpleasant to produce results. But it should be keyed to the requirements of racing and to individual tastes and needs.

Basically, cross country ski racers follow a year-round training program similar to that used by long-distance foot runners, with the addition of special skiing exercises. But training for cross country ski racing is difficult to regiment. Race-course profiles are seldom identical, and the terrain variations encountered make it impossible to single out any one strength or ability that is most important. The most important physiological abilities required are aerobic capacity (the ability to work when supplied with oxygen), and anaerobic capacity (the ability to work for shorter periods of time without oxygen). Cross country ski racing is mostly an endurance event involving aerobic work, but it also has many anaerobic periods, such as when a racer runs hills, or sprints at a start or finish. Muscular fitness, involving strength and resilience, must also be trained to provide the capabilities needed in racing.

The training necessary to produce these capabilities is divided up into distance, interval, tempos and strength training. *Distance training* is a continuously paced foot running or skiing exercise of at least half, and usually not more than twice, the duration of a ski race. Its purpose is to maintain or increase the body's ability to use its aerobic capacity. When distance training, you should pace yourself to move steadily throughout the exercise period. Two checks on speed are that you should be able to talk to a running mate without getting out of breath, and you should be able to speed up at any time. If you cannot do one or both of these, slow down—you're going too fast to realize the benefit of distance training.

*Interval training* is a skiing stride, foot- or skiing-run comprising a series of intense but relatively short exercise periods, from tens of seconds to a few minutes, separated from one another by rest intervals of shorter duration. Its purpose is to maintain or increase aerobic capacity. There are two main types of interval training: *timed interval,* in which sprints and rests follow a definite timed sequence on a track or up and down a single hill, and *natural interval,* as done in undulating terrain with uphills and downhills providing exercise loads equivalent to sprints and rests. When interval training, you should pace yourself to maintain the same speed in all sprints of an exercise period. A check on the effectiveness of your sprint speed is that you should feel just slightly stiff and slightly out of breath towards the end of each sprint. If you feel stiff during the sprints, you're going too fast.

*Tempo training* is running or skiing at racing speeds or greater, using the sprint-rest interval sequence of exercise. Its purpose is to maintain or increase anaerobic capacity (often called "oxygen debt") and build sprint ability. Tempo speed should be such that you feel stiff at the end of each sprint. You can also time yourself to check speed.

*Strength training* builds the muscles used in racing. All strength training should be done with cross country racing in mind. Powerful muscles capable of slowly exerting great force are useless in cross country ski racing where rapid, explosive, repetitive movements are needed. There are two types of strength training: *stationary*, such as indoor gym exercise, and *moving*, such as simulating ski movements on foot. Both aim mostly at strengthening weak muscle groups or, in most cases, muscle groups otherwise neglected in summer running and hiking. There are two types of stationary exercises: those using body weight alone and those using apparatus or weights. Those using body weight alone are the most easily done. Foremost are exercises for the abdomen and back, the muscle groups that connect arms and legs when you ski. Exercises using weights are beneficial, but the total weight used in regular workouts should be limited by what you can move with the same rapid movements as in skiing.

Situps with knees bent strengthen abdominal muscles used in skiing.

## Imitation Training

Off-snow training that exercises skiing muscles in the same motions and body joints and in the same angles as in skiing is imitation training. Because cross country uses both arms and legs, while foot running uses only legs, all skiing training should incorporate some imitation training. The most common imitation exercises are arm exercises, uphill ski striding, and roller skiing.

*Arm exercises* use resistance devices or elastics to exercise arms in poling movements. They are used primarily for strength training. Resistance devices, such as cords running through braking devices, most closely approximate the load of pole movements. Elastics, which give an increasing resistance, provide the opposite of actual skiing pole resistance.

*Ski striding* is moving uphill to simulate the resistance of skiing. It may be done at a fast walk or at a bounding run, with or without poles. The most important characteristics of good ski striding are rapid and complete leg extensions on each kick, and good rhythm and balance. The bounding run version with poles is shown here.

*Roller skiing* simulates cross-country skiing on paved surfaces, using roller skis, which resemble giant roller skates. Roller skis attach to the feet

## Arm Exercises

Arm exercises with resistance devices or elastic cords build poling muscles.

with racing bindings and boots, and usually have three wheels with hard-rubber tires, one or more fitted with a ratchet that prevents backward motion, to simulate on-snow ski grip. Most roller skis are about 48 mm wide, slightly wider than racing skis, but weigh about 6½ pounds a pair, more than double the weight of a pair of racing skis and bindings.

### The training year

Complete training programs should be tailored to suit individual needs, both in the amount and type of training. No concise program can suit all racers. As a guide, however, the year can be divided into four training seasons whose major activities are: off season, build-up, change-over, and racing.

### Uphill Ski Stride

The kick is short and arms duplicate diagonal stride movements.

| Training season | Distance | Interval | Tempo | Strength | Roller Skiing | Total hrs per week |
|---|---|---|---|---|---|---|
| Spring-summer | 5-7 | 0-1 | 0 | 2 | 1-1½ | 7-9½ |
| Autumn | 6-8 | 1-2 | 0 | 1-2 | 2½-3 | 10½-15 |
| Early winter | 10-14 | 1-2 | 0 | 0 | 0 | 11-16 |
| Winter | 2-3 + races | 2-3 | 1 | 0 | 0 | 5-7 + races |

Average minimum weekly training hours for adult cross country ski racers. Hyphenated numbers indicate increase in hours from start to end of training season.

*Spring-summer, off-season:* Distance training dominates, taking about three-quarters of training time. Interval training accounts for a little under a quarter, and increases towards the end of the period. Do a little strength training, working on any specially weak muscle groups. Many cross country racers compete in summer track or other athletic events, both for training and to break the routine of cross country programs.

*Autumn, build-up:* At the beginning, distance training dominates, but at the end interval training accounts for almost half of training time. Tempo training should start towards the end of the period.

*Early winter, change-over:* This is the transition period when you must become accustomed to skiing. Emphasis is on special ski training. Distance and interval training continue, but tempo and on-ski technique training become increasingly important.

*Winter, skiing:* Initially no more than one or two races a week, but often more towards the end of the period. Distance and interval training continue in amounts suited to individual condition and racing schedules. Tempo training is gradually phased out, although some racers use short races as tempo training for longer, more important events.

A training program typical of that followed by adult racers is shown in the table. The adult training schedule is, of course, more demanding than

Roller skis resemble giant roller skates.
Their front wheels have ratchets to
prevent rolling backwards.

Almost all skiing strides can be done on roller skis.

that for younger skiers, simply because adults race longer distances at higher speeds. As an approximate guide, teenage youths should train about half to two-thirds as much as adults, depending on age.

**Training Testing**
The true test of effective training is whether or not skiing times improve. However, physiological testing is useful as a check during a training season. Many tests are used, of which the Ergometer cycle is the most common and most easily administered. In the Ergometer test, the subject pedals a stationary cycle at a constant speed against a resistance. The measured

Off-season training on ski trails
builds feeling for terrain.

pulse rate and body weight then give an index of the maximum oxygen uptake, which is a direct indication of aerobic capacity, the most important ability in cross country ski racing. Ergometer cycles are standard team equipment for most major cross country racing teams.

## Courses and Regulations

Standard international cross country courses are laid out in rolling terrain with climbs, downhills, turns and flats to challenge the skiers' technique, condition and tactics. A terrain profile of a course indicates its difficulty. A race course laid out and maintained according to the FIS (International Ski Federation) specifications allows racers to fairly pit their abilities against each other. The complete FIS regulations are too lengthy to repeat here; they are available from all national ski associations.

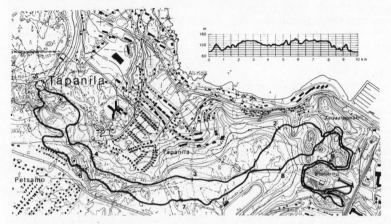

Typical course: The 1978 FIS World Ski Championship men's 4 x 10 km relay course profile, Lahti, Finland.

The maximum permissible lengths of races in most countries depend on the racers' ages and sex. There is no age limit for cross country participants in World Ski Championships; the national ski associations are responsible for the preparation of their racers. Cross country course difficulty can be stated in terms of the total amount of climbing, or total elevation gain, around a course. The standards for elevation gain are:

| Course | Total elevation gain should be in the range | Typical course: 1978 FIS World Ski Championships, Lahti, Finland |
|---|---|---|
| 5km women's | 150-200m (492-656 ft) | 180m (590 ft) |
| 10km women's | 250-350m (820-1148 ft) | 290m (951 ft) |
| 20km women's | 400-500m (1312-1640 ft) | 490m (1607 ft) |
| 10km men's | 300-450m (984-1476 ft) | 280m (918 ft) |
| 15km men's | 450-600m (1476-1968 ft) | 485m (1590 ft) |
| 30km men's | 750-1,000m (2460-3280 ft) | 820m (2689 ft) |
| 50km men's | 1,200-1,500m (3936-4920 ft) | 1435m (4707 ft) |

The maximum permissible elevation for an FIS-approved course is 1,650 meters (5,412 ft.) above sea level. Relays, combined cross country and the biathlon complete the list of cross country racing events.

*Relays:* Men's relays are 4 x 10km and women's are 4 x 5km. Total elevation gains are the same as for individual courses of the same length. The courses must be laid out with multiple tracks.

*Combined:* The cross country race course for the Nordic combined, which also includes ski jumping from a 70 meter hill, is 15km, and has the same general specifications as for the 15km special course.

*Biathlon:* The individual biathlon event comprises four shooting bouts on a 20km cross country course, while the 4 x 7.5km relay comprises two shooting bouts on each lap. Courses are often laid out in loops to use one common range for all shooting. Biathlon is a Winter Olympic, but not an FIS event; it is organized by the UIPMB (International Modern Pentathlon and Biathlon Association).

## The Big Events

Major international ski competition started with two cross country events, the 18km and 50km men's races, and ski jumping in the first Winter Olympic Games, held in Chamonix, France in 1924.

The Winter Olympic Games, held in leap years, now has four cross country events for men: 15, 30 and 50km individual and 4 x 10km relay; four cross country events for women: 5, 10 and 20km individual and 4 x 5km relay; plus the Nordic combined and two biathlon events. The FIS World Ski Championships, held on even-numbered years between Winter Olympic Games, has the same events in cross country, except biathlon, not an FIS event. Winter Olympic Games are numbered, starting with the first in Chamonix: the 1980 Winter Olympics, scheduled for Lake Placid, will be the 13th. The Winter Olympic events count as World Ski Championships, and are numbered along with FIS WSC Games: the 1978 FIS World Ski Championships in Lahti, Finland are the 32nd, while the thirteenth Winter Olympic Games counts as FIS Championships number 33.

The Cross Country World Cup, approved in 1977 by the FIS on a trial basis for 1978-79 and 1980-81, is scheduled for every second winter when there is no Winter Olympics or World Championships. The World Cup is based on point totals earned by racers' five best results out of nine major international FIS races during the season: 15, 30 and 50km events for men, 5, 10 and 20km events for women. First place in a race earns 26 points, second 22, third 19, fourth 17, fifth 16, and so on by one-point increments down to 20th, which earns one point. The theoretical maximum is five firsts, or 130 points.

## Citizens' Racing

No discussion of racing is complete without mention of citizens' races, those events in which the goal for most is not win, but to participate. Although top racers usually enter and win the major citizens' races, these events are primarily for recreational skiers. Most have several classes, broken down by age, sex and skiing ability. The major citizens' races have prizes for the top placings plus medals or certificates for all who finish within fixed percentages of the winning time, with percentages varying according to class in the race. The races are usually mass-start events, with multiple tracks set for the first few hundred yards.

Distances vary according to the race. The largest and oldest citizens'

The relay is cross country ski racing's "sprint" event (Tim Caldwell tags Bill Koch, US team in 1978 FIS 4 x 10 km relay, Lahti, Finland).

Biathlon combines shooting and cross country racing (1976 Winter Olympics, Seefeld, Austria).

race is the *Vasaloppet* in Sweden, which was originated in 1922. Each year 10,000 or more skiers line up in Sälen to ski to Mora, re-tracing the route taken in 1521 by Swedish patriot (and later king) Gustaf Vasa. The best time over the route was set in 1979 at 4 hours, 5 minutes and 58 seconds, an average of 2 minutes 52 seconds per kilometer, or 4 minutes 39½ seconds per mile. The world's longest citizens' race is the Canadian Ski Marathon, an informal event in which racers and tourers may ski as little as 20 or as much as 100 miles, in two days. Those who manage 50 miles a

The American Birkebeiner is one of the major US citizens' races.

day for the two days are called *Les Coureurs de Bois*—literally "Runners of the Woods." Throughout the US and Canada, hundreds of citizens' races are arranged every season. In Europe they are an established part of the winter competitive scene. Entries to citizens' races are usually informal, requiring no more than filling out an entry blank and paying a modest fee. For longer events, advance entry is usually required, and many races require medical certificates of good health.

Serious citizens' racers train by the same principles used by competitive racers. However, as shown in the table, they train less—which suits their recreational approach to the sport.

| Training season | Distance | Interval | Strength | Misc. training, such as roller skiing | Total hrs per week |
|---|---|---|---|---|---|
| Spring-summer | 3-5 | 0-½ | ½-1 | 0-1 | 3½-7½ |
| Autumn | 4-6 | ½-1 | 1 | 1 | 6½-9 |
| Early winter | 6-8 | ½-1 | 0 | 0 | 6½-9 |
| Winter | 3-4 + one race | 1-1½ | 0 | 0 | 4-5½ |

**Average weekly training hours for serious adult citizens' racers. Hyphenated numbers indicate increase in hours from start to end of training season.**

## The King of Sports

Cross country ski racing, like cross country skiing in general, offers something for almost every competitive ability, and knows no economic or social boundaries. There are even citizens' races for those who otherwise could not enjoy competition: the *Ridderennet* (Race of the Knights) in

In the "Race for Light", sighted skiers guide the blind racers.

Norway and the *Race for Light* in the U.S. annually attract blind and handicapped skiers from all over the world. This universal nature of cross country ski racing may be why it's often called the king of winter sports. In any case, it is the only competitive winter sport in which a modern king has competed: on March 6, 1977 Sweden's King Carl XVI Gustav showed up among the 11,527 skiers starting in the Vasaloppet and finished in the top half of the 85.6km event as number 5708, beating more than 5,000 of his countrymen.

King Carl XVI Gustav of Sweden in the 1977 Vasaloppet citizens' race. He beat more than 5000 of his countrymen in the event.

Photo and Drawing Credits: M.M. Brady: 6, 8, 71, 73, 74, 85; Studio 9: 9;
Organizing Committee, 1978 FIS Nordic World Ski Championships: 83; Telemark
Lodge: 86; Woodstock Inn: 87; Pressens Bild: 87. Otherwise all photography by Frits
Solvang; all drawings by Odd Pettersen.